PREPARATORY COURSE FOR THE
ASWB BACHELORS LEVEL EXAM

Professional Relationships, Values, and Ethics

**Association for Advanced Training
in the Behavioral Sciences**
212 W. Ironwood Drive, Suite D #168 Coeur d'Alene, ID 83814
(800) 472-1931

© Association for Advanced Training in the Behavioral Sciences. All rights reserved. No part of these materials may be reproduced in any form, or by any means, mechanical or electronic, including photocopying, without the written permission of the publisher. To reproduce or adapt, in whole or in part, any portion of these materials is not only a violation of copyright law, but is unethical and unprofessional. As a condition of your acceptance of these materials, you agree not to reproduce or adapt them in any manner or license others to do so. The unauthorized resale of these materials is prohibited. The Association for Advanced Training in the Behavioral Sciences accepts the responsibility of protecting not only its own interests, but to protect the interests of its authors and to maintain and vigorously enforce all copyrights on its material. Your cooperation in complying with the copyright law is appreciated.

BACHELORS LEVEL

PROFESSIONAL RELATIONSHIPS, VALUES, AND ETHICS

Table of Contents

I. Professional Values and Ethics 1
  A. Introduction 1
  B. Confidentiality 5
  C. Client Self-Determination 20
  D. Competence 22
  E. Informed Consent 26
  F. Payment for Services 29
  G. Conflicts of Interest and Dual/Multiple Relationships 31
  H. Clients' Access to Their Records 34
  I. Client Transfer: Potential Client Receiving Services From a Colleague 35
  J. Interruption or Termination of Services 36
  K. Representing and Advertising Your Services 37
  L. Other Professional Issues 38

II. Social Worker Roles in Interventions with Clients/Client Systems 46

III. The Social Worker-Client Relationship – Professional Use of Self 49
  A. Conditions for Effective Helping Relationships 49
  B. Responding to Client Behavior That May Impede Acceptance 51
  C. Demonstrating Your Authenticity 54
  D. Transference and Countertransference 57

IV. Supervision in Social Work 59
  A. Overview of Supervision 59
  B. Individual Supervision and Group Supervision 63
  C. Supervision Procedures 66
  D. Administrative Supervision 68
  E. Educational Supervision 74
  F. Supportive Supervision 76
  G. Evaluation/Performance Appraisal 79
  H. Miscellaneous Topics Related to Supervision 83

Appendix I: Summary of the NASW Code of Ethics 85

The NASW Code of Ethics (NASW, 2017) 85
Appendix II: Professional Standards of the NASW 111

BACHELORS LEVEL

PROFESSIONAL RELATIONSHIPS, VALUES, AND ETHICS

NOTES: The information presented in this chapter is for informational purposes only and is not meant to serve as ethical or legal advice. For ethical or legal advice, please contact a professional organization, state licensing board, or attorney.

The use of pronouns is extensive in our study material. To avoid cumbersome phrasing and simplify your reading, we use primarily masculine pronouns in some chapters and primarily feminine pronouns in others.

I. Professional Values and Ethics

"Values" are "customs, standards, and principles considered desirable by a culture, a group of people, or an individual" (Barker, 2003, p. 453). "Ethical standards," in contrast, serve as a guide to what is right versus wrong and relate to how we conduct ourselves in a professional context. While values are abstract, ethics tend to be codified into a formal system or set of rules that are explicitly adopted by a group of people.

A. Introduction

NASW Code of Ethics

As part of its activities in establishing and maintaining standards of social work practice, the National Association of Social Workers (NASW) has developed and adopted a Code of Ethics for the profession. The NASW Code of Ethics (hereafter referred to as "the Code of Ethics" or "the Code") summarizes broad **ethical principles** that reflect social work's core values as well as establishes a set of **ethical standards** that social workers should use to guide their professional actions.

The Code of Ethics serves the following purposes (NASW, 2017):

- It identifies the fundamental values upon which your mission as a social worker is based.

- It summarizes broad ethical principles that reflect the profession's core values and establishes a set of specific ethical standards that you should use to guide your social work practice.

- It is designed to help you identify relevant considerations when professional obligations conflict or ethical uncertainties arise.

- It provides ethical standards to which the general public can hold the social work profession accountable.
- It socializes practitioners new to the field to social work's mission, values, ethical principles, and ethical standards.
- It articulates standards that the social work profession can use to assess whether social workers have engaged in unethical conduct.

Social workers affirm the Code of Ethics when they join the NASW and abide by it because they are committed to advancing the highest standards of social work practice. Even if you are not a member of NASW, you may be bound by its ethical code in malpractice cases. The Code applies not only to social workers but also social work students. In addition, social workers must follow the Code, regardless of the professional functions they perform, the settings they work in, or the populations they serve.

All social workers who have affirmed the Code of Ethics are required to cooperate in its application and abide by all disciplinary actions based on it. In addition, social workers should take adequate steps to prevent, discourage, correct, and expose the unethical behavior of their colleagues as well as defend and help colleagues who are unfairly accused of ethical misconduct.

1. The Code of Ethics and Professional Values: The core **professional values** considered desirable by social workers include the following: (a) a commitment to the primary importance of the individual in society; (b) respect for the confidentiality of relationships with clients; (c) a commitment to social change to meet socially recognized needs; (d) a willingness to keep personal feelings and needs separate from professional relationships; (e) a willingness to transmit knowledge and skills to others; (f) respect and appreciation for individual and group differences; (g) a commitment to develop clients' ability to help themselves; (h) a willingness to persist in efforts on behalf of a client despite frustration; (i) a commitment to social justice and the economic, physical, and mental well-being of all persons in society; and (j) a commitment to a high standard of personal and professional conduct.

These values are incorporated in the Code of Ethics so that behaving in an ethical manner is a way of realizing the fundamental values of your profession. The Code summarizes these values in the following way:

Service: As a social worker, your primary goal is "to help people in need and to address social problems."

Social justice: You challenge social injustice and work to bring about social change with and on behalf of individuals and groups, especially those who are vulnerable and oppressed.

Dignity and worth of the person: You respect the inherent dignity and worth of the person (e.g., you treat each person in a compassionate and respectful way, respect cultural and ethnic differences, and promote your clients' self-determination whenever it is socially responsible to do so).

Importance of human relationships: You recognize the central importance of human relationships (e.g., you engage your clients and others who receive your services as partners in the helping process).

Integrity: You behave in a trustworthy manner.

Competence: You practice within your areas of competence and develop and enhance your professional expertise.

STUDY TIP: In Appendix I of this chapter, we paraphrase all of the values, principles, and standards contained in the Code of Ethics. To prepare for the ethics questions on the exam, we recommend that you become very familiar with the Code of Ethics. You do NOT need to memorize the Code word-for-word or to know the numbers and letters associated with the standards (e.g., Standard 1.08, section a), but you should become familiar enough with the Code that you can apply its provisions to concrete situations (i.e., the ethical dilemmas presented in exam questions). This is fairly easy to do if you keep in mind the professional values that underlie the Code of Ethics.

2. When Ethics Conflict With Laws or Policies: If you encounter a situation in which your ethical responsibilities conflict with a law or regulation or the policies or procedures of the agency where you work, you must, according to the Code of Ethics, make a good-faith effort to resolve the conflict. Whatever resolution you come to must be consistent with the principles and standards set forth in the Code of Ethics. If a resolution that is consistent with the Code of Ethics is impossible, you should seek **consultation** before making a final decision. In making such a decision, it is important to provide detailed documentation regarding the ethical reasoning leading to the decision. In addition, remember that the actions you undertake in your professional capacity will often be judged by a **reasonable standard of care** criterion (i.e., what a reasonable person in a similar situation would do).

a. Conflict Between Ethics and Laws: A difficult dilemma arises when adherence to an ethical standard violates a law or regulation. In these situations, you should (a) make known your commitment to the Code of Ethics and (b) take steps to resolve the conflict in a responsible manner. This does *not* mean you should violate a law or regulation. Indeed, you must comply with the laws and regulations that govern your practice. Instead, as an ethical social worker, you should handle such conflicts by making every effort to ensure that ethical standards are upheld to the greatest extent possible and working toward ensuring that laws and regulations are consistent with ethical requirements.

b. Conflict Between Ethics and Policies or Procedures: As a social worker, you must ordinarily comply with the policies and procedures of the agency that employs you as well as those of other organizations and voluntary associations, but when a policy is unjust or otherwise harms the well-being of clients or colleagues, you *may* be justified in violating it. One example of this, according to Hepworth (2006), is a policy or practice that exploits or discriminates against individuals or groups. For instance, if your agency made it a practice, following screening, to select only relatively healthy or financially well-to-do clients and to refuse services to individuals not meeting these criteria (a practice called "cherry picking" or "creaming"), then you would be justified in concluding that the well-being of the adversely affected individuals takes precedence over your obligation to comply with this policy.

The Code of Ethics (Standard 3.09) addresses situations in which ethical standards conflict with institutional or organizational/agency policies or regulations by explicitly stating that you should NOT allow your employing organization's policies, procedures, regulations, or administrative orders to interfere with your ethical practice of social work. Instead, to uphold ethical standards to the highest degree possible, you should ensure that your employer is aware of your ethical obligations and the implications of these obligations for your practice as a social worker and that your employing organization's practices are consistent with the Code of Ethics. Furthermore, you should work to eliminate any conditions in the organization that violate, interfere with, or discourage compliance with the Code of Ethics.

TEST-TAKING TIP: Do not take into consideration the unique policies of an organization where you work (or at which you worked in the past) when answering exam questions. Agency policies vary widely and cannot be the subject of ASWB exam questions.

3. When Ethics Conflict With Personal Values: When a work-related situation presents a conflict between your professional and personal values, you must deal with the conflict in a responsible way: If the situation or action is morally uncomfortable for you, but consistent with the Code of Ethics (and/or a law), you should put aside your discomfort, seek supervision and/or consultation, and if needed, follow the Code of Ethics (and/or law).

4. Bioethics: "Bioethics" involves the philosophical study of ethical controversies arising from advances in biology and medicine. The field addresses a wide range of issues, including debates over the boundaries of life (e.g., abortion, euthanasia), surrogacy, the allocation of scarce health-care resources, experimentation with human subjects, behavioral control (e.g., through the use of psychotropic medications), and the right to turn down medical care for religious or cultural reasons. Principles contained in the Belmont Report (1979) have influenced the thinking of bioethicists across a wide range of issues. This document outlines ethical principles and guidelines for the protection of human subjects of research. Many of these principles – autonomy, respect for persons, beneficence (doing good), and justice – are consistent with core values underlying social work practice.

5. The Code of Ethics as the Basis for Adjudication in Matters of Ethics: An important function of the Code of Ethics is to serve as the basis for adjudication in matters of ethics when a social worker is alleged to have violated an ethical standard.

The NASW has established formal procedures to adjudicate ethics complaints filed against social workers who are NASW members. When an NASW member is accused of ethical misconduct, the matter is subject to a **peer review** process. A complaint may be heard and adjudicated by a committee known as a **committee on inquiry (NASW Ethics Committee)**. This committee looks into the alleged ethical violation to determine if any wrong-doing has occurred. The committee then reports its findings to the NASW's Board of Directors. Punishments, known as **professional sanctions**, are imposed when a social worker is found to have committed an ethical violation. The most common punishments imposed on social workers who are NASW members include required retraining and counseling for a specified period of time, public notification of the violation, probation of the social worker's NASW membership status, and expulsion from the NASW.

Note that a social worker who has committed an ethical violation is not necessarily guilty of breaking the law and will not always be tried in a legal proceeding. Instead, determination of legal liability has to take place in a legal context. All legal processes as well as administrative procedures stemming from ethical violations by social workers are kept separate from the peer review process so that the social work profession can advise and discipline its own members.

6. Responding to a Colleague's Unethical Behavior: The Code of Ethics (Standard 2.10) requires you to respond to ethical violations by social work colleagues. The primary reason why the Code requires this is to protect clients and the public from unethical social workers, including from the harm that may result from a social worker's unethical behavior.

The Code of Ethics allows social workers to use their discretion in determining the best course of action in cases where they suspect a colleague of behaving unethically: Depending on which course of action they deem to be most appropriate, social workers can either (a) attempt to resolve the colleague's ethical infraction informally or (b) use more formal channels by filing a complaint. Usually a social worker would try to seek resolution of the problem informally by discussing his concerns with the colleague. This approach is appropriate when the discussion is feasible and is likely to be productive. When the colleague's unethical conduct is not appropriate for informal resolution – for instance, the discussion is not likely to be productive or the violation is harming a client in a serious way – a social worker should take action through designated formal channels, which usually involves contacting a state licensing board or regulatory body, the NASW Ethics Committee, or other professional ethics committee.

When deciding how to respond to a colleague's unethical conduct, a social worker must also consider the question of **confidentiality**. For example, if a client told you that her former social worker borrowed a large sum of money from her and hasn't paid her back and that he came to therapy sessions drunk, you could not report this behavior to anyone without having a signed release from the client. Also, in this situation, the better course of action would be to first let the client decide if she wants to file a complaint herself.

Professional Standards of the NASW

In addition to a Code of Ethics, NASW has established numerous sets of professional standards, which serve as important guidelines for professional social workers in a variety of practice settings. These standards include the Standards for Continuing Professional Education; Standards for the Practice of Clinical Social Work; Standards for the Classification of Social Work Practice; Standards for the Practice of Social Work with Adolescents; Standards of Practice for Social Work Mediators; Standards for School Social Work Services; Standards for Social Work Case Management; Standards for Social Work in Health Care Settings; Standards for Social Work Personnel Practices; Standards for Social Work Practice in Child Protection; Standards for Social Work Services in Long-Term Care Facilities; and Standards for the Use of Technology. According to the NASW, you should interpret all of these standards within the ethical foundation and values expressed in the Code of Ethics.

In Appendix II of this chapter, we excerpt and paraphrase many of the professional standards established by the NASW. You should become familiar with the general requirements of these documents, but they are not as important for the exam as the Code of Ethics.

B. Confidentiality

Definition of Privacy, Confidentiality, and Privilege

1. Privacy: Privacy refers to the basic right of an individual to decide how much personal information can be shared with others. The Code of Ethics (Standard 1.07) requires you to respect your clients' rights to privacy. This means that you should not ask for private information from a client unless you need the information to provide your services or conduct social work evaluation or research.

2. Confidentiality: Confidentiality is based on the right to privacy, but is narrower and refers to your obligation not to disclose any information about a client, research or evaluation subject, supervisee, employee, etc., obtained during the course of a professional relationship without the person's permission. Of course, a client's right to confidentiality is not absolute. There are times when it is ethical to disclose confidential information about a client; these situations will be discussed in this section.

3. Privilege: Privilege is also derived from privacy and is a legal right that prevents confidential information from being disclosed in a court or other legal proceeding without the permission of the person or her legal representative.

In most situations, the client is the **holder of the privilege**; that is, the client must sign a waiver before a social worker or other professional can release confidential information about her in a legal proceeding. An exception to this general rule occurs when a client is a minor (under age 18) or legally incompetent (e.g., mentally disabled). In these cases, the parent or legal guardian is essentially the holder of the privilege – that is, the parent or legal guardian has the right to "waive" or "claim" the privilege on behalf of the client.

Finally, while privilege and confidentiality are often treated as separate issues, there is a great deal of overlap. The word "confidentiality" appears in many state laws, and, in some states, a client has a legal right to sue a social worker for a breach of confidentiality.

NOTE: The laws that define the limits of privilege vary from state to state, and your knowledge of state laws is not tested on an ASWB exam.

Maintaining Confidentiality

After you obtain private information from a client, the standards of confidentiality apply. Confidentiality is addressed in Standard 1.07 (a-w) of the Code of Ethics. In general, you must protect the confidentiality of all information you obtain in the course of your professional service, although an exception to this occurs when there is a **compelling professional reason** to disclose the information (see Disclosing Confidential Information Without Valid Consent, below). And, to further ensure that your clients' privacy and confidentiality are protected, you should provide confidential information only to people clearly connected with a client's case.

1. Guidelines Specified in Ethical Standard 1.07: The Code of Ethics (Standard 1.07) provides guidelines for maintaining confidentiality in specific situations, including those described below.

a. Family and Couples Counseling and Therapy: When providing family or couples counseling or therapy, you should, as early as possible in the relationship, seek an agreement from the participants to maintain one another's confidentiality and also inform them that you cannot guarantee that all of the participants will honor this agreement.

In family or couples counseling or therapy, the problem of "**secrets**" can arise. This problem is especially likely to occur if you also see one member of a family or one or both members of a couple in a private session. For instance, a wife might disclose during a private session that she is having an affair. What should you do in this situation? This is a complex issue, and to help avoid such dilemmas, you should, as soon as possible in the relationship, clearly state your own position as well as your employer's or agency's policy with regard to keeping or sharing "secrets." Corey, Corey, and Callahan have suggested that the best policy is to let clients know that information given in private sessions "will be divulged as ... [social workers] see fit in accordance with the greatest benefit for the couple or the family" (1988, p. 307).

b. Group Counseling and Therapy: At the beginning of group counseling or group therapy, you should seek an agreement from all of the participants to maintain one another's confidentiality, ideally in writing. When seeking this agreement, you should also inform the group members that you cannot guarantee that all of the participants will abide by the agreement. This is important to do because the members of a counseling or therapy group are not ethically or legally required to maintain the confidentiality of what they hear from other members during group meetings. You should also inform the members of your own, your employer's, and your agency's policy regarding whether or not and when you will disclose confidential information among the clients involved in the group counseling or therapy.

c. Consultation: When seeking consultation, you should not disclose *identifying* information about a client unless you have obtained signed permission from the client or there is a compelling need to disclose such information. Furthermore, you should share with the consultant only relevant information; specifically, you should share only information that is necessary to achieve the purpose(s) of the consultation. Note that an implication of this ethical standard is that it is not necessary to get a client's permission to discuss her case with a consultant as long as you do not disclose information that would reveal the client's identity to the consultant.

d. Third-Party Payers: You should not disclose confidential information to third-party payers (e.g., insurance companies, Medicare) unless the client has authorized you to do so.

e. Legal Proceedings: To the degree permitted by law, you should protect the confidentiality of your clients during legal proceedings. If a legally authorized body, such as a court of law, orders you to disclose confidential or privileged information without a client's consent and you believe that such disclosure could result in harm to the client, you should: (a) ask the court to withdraw the order; (b) try to limit the order as narrowly as possible; or (c) ask the court to keep the relevant records under seal, where they are unavailable for public inspection. (See also Responding to a Subpoena, later in this section.)

f. Deceased Clients: You should protect the confidentiality of deceased clients in a manner consistent with confidentiality standards found in the Code of Ethics and governing law. This means that you should not release confidential information after a client's death without proper authorization (e.g., a release from the executor of the client's estate or the client's legal representative).

g. Preparing Written Records and Oral Reports: You must minimize invasions of privacy by including only relevant information in written records and oral reports. For example, in written records, you should document only information that is directly relevant to the delivery of services.

h. Public Media: The Code of Ethics requires you to avoid including identifying information about clients, students, research subjects, etc., in lectures, writings, and other public media unless you have obtained permission from the person to do so. For example, if a social worker who is both a counselor and a professor at a university substantiates his class lectures with examples of students he has treated in the school's counseling center, he would have to avoid presenting any information that would reveal a student's identity to the class. The Code of Ethics also requires you to protect the confidentiality of your clients when responding to requests from members of the media.

i. Storing Written and Electronic Records: Protecting the confidentiality of your clients' written and electronic records and other sensitive information requires you to (a) take reasonable steps to make sure that clients' records are stored in a secure place and are not available to others who are not authorized to obtain or read them, and (b) transfer or dispose of clients' records in a way that protects their confidentiality and is consistent with your state's statutes concerning records and social work licensure.

j. Transmission of Information Using Electronic or Computer Technology: You must take steps to guarantee and maintain the confidentiality of information transmitted to others through the use of computers, e-mail, fax machines, telephones, telephone answering machines, voicemail, and other electronic or computer technology. It is the responsibility of the social worker to be aware of the risks involved in using technology. You must document and maintain all client information in a secure location, protected by safeguards. When transmitting information using electronic or computer technology, you should, whenever possible, avoid disclosing identifying information about a client. If you do have a written release to disclose identifying information protected by HIPAA, the software used for storage and transmission must be HIPAA compliant.

k. Teaching and Training: Unless a client has consented to disclosure of confidential information, you should not reveal identifying information when discussing a client for teaching or training purposes. (See also Public Media, above on this list.)

In addition, you should not talk about confidential information in any setting (electronically or in-person) in which privacy cannot be guaranteed (for example, you should not discuss confidential information in public or semi-public areas such as hallways, waiting rooms, elevators and restaurants); and you must take reasonable steps to protect your clients' confidetiality in the event of your termination of practice, incapacitation, or death.

Finally, while confidentiality is commonly thought of in terms of the information that a client reveals in therapy, it also refers to **keeping the fact of the relationship confidential**. In other words, inquiries as to whether a person is your client should ordinarily be answered by telling the inquirer that client identities are not disclosed.

2. Additional Guidelines: Of course, confidentiality standards also apply in professional situations that are not directly discussed in Standard 1.07. Examples of these situations and how to handle them in an ethical manner are discussed below.

a. Clients Who are Court-Ordered: Typically, when a client is **court-ordered** (ordered by the court to receive therapy), the court (a) requires that the client attend a certain number of sessions as a condition of her probation, parole, or sentence; (b) determines what information the therapist may not keep confidential; and (c) requires that the client sign a release of information that permits her therapist to inform the court about whether or not the client complies with the court order. The client may choose not to comply with a court request for the release of information, but in doing so may be held in contempt of court. Therefore, even when a court has ordered a client to receive services, the client's right to confidentiality is NOT waived: You need to have a release of information signed by the client in order to discuss her case with others, including court personnel or her probation officer. The same is true if a court-ordered client is on parole; you would need a release of information signed by the client in order to discuss anything with her parole officer.

b. Attorney Request for a Client Records: As an ethical social worker, you should not release a client's records based on just a request from an attorney without having consent from the client to do so. Instead, you should take steps to protect the client's confidentiality to the greatest extent permitted by law. With this in mind, your first step would be to assert the privilege on your client's behalf and not release her records. You would then want to discuss the attorney's request with the client and, if relevant, the client's attorney, including the possible consequences of releasing the records to the attorney. If the client ends up signing a release (waiving the privilege), you can then provide the records. You may not however release any third party information that has been obtained as part of the record. If the client refuses to sign the release, you need to continue asserting the privilege on the client's behalf. The issue could then end up in court, and a judge might issue an order requiring you to release the records. (For more information on this, see Responding to a Subpoena, later in this section.)

c. Malpractice Cases: First of all, for a client or other person to bring a claim of **malpractice** against a therapist, three conditions must be met: (a) The therapist had a professional relationship with the person, which established a legal duty of care; (b) the therapist has breached that duty by acting in a way not consistent with the expected standard of care (e.g., by acting negligently); and (c) as a direct result of the breach of duty, the person has suffered harm. The therapist's actions do not have to have been malevolent, but there must be evidence that the therapist's actions are the cause of the harm suffered by the client.

Malpractice cases are civil suits that require a plaintiff (the client) to prove her claim by a "preponderance of the evidence." In other words, the plaintiff must establish a standard of care and show that the defendant (the therapist) did not meet it. Because confidential information may be necessary or relevant to the therapist's defense, the therapist can disclose relevant confidential information during the legal proceeding, and the client cannot invoke the privilege to prevent the information from being admitted into the legal proceeding.

Finally, a social worker sued for malpractice may be asked to attend a **deposition**. As a defendant, the social worker would have to comply with this request. Depositions are one part of the legal process called "discovery." During discovery, one party in a lawsuit discovers facts and information from another party in a lawsuit. The facts and information allow the parties to identify the issues that will be addressed during the trial. Depositions consist of oral questions and answers (an "interrogatory" is the written equivalent of a deposition). Testimony at a deposition takes place under oath and is recorded by a court reporter.

d. Adjudication Procedures for Ethical Violations: As a social worker, you must cooperate fully and in a timely fashion with the adjudication procedures of the committee of inquiry, peer review, and the state board. However, a complaint by a client to a licensing board or other professional association does not, in and of itself, grant the social worker the right to discuss the client's case or release the client's records. Instead, when responding to such a complaint, you should disclose confidential information only if the client has signed a release. By filing a complaint, a client has, in most cases, given permission for her records to be released – your obligation, then, would be to verify this before disclosing confidential information or releasing the records. (Particularly if you are the target of the client's complaint, it's also a good idea to hire a lawyer, preferably one with experience before regulatory boards, to assist you in handling your response to the complaint.)

Finally, if a licensing board or other professional association asks you for your records on a client (and the client has authorized their release), it would be inappropriate for you to summarize the records before submitting them.

e. Case Management: NASW's Standards for Social Work Case Management state that case managers, like all social workers, must protect a client's right to privacy and appropriate confidentiality. You should explain confidentiality and its limits to the client, discuss that effective case management requires an exchange of information about the client between the members of her helping network, and get signed releases of information from the client.

Of course, informal helpers, such as family or friends, are not bound by ethical standards or laws that require them to protect a client's right to privacy and confidentiality. Many case managers make decisions about sharing confidential information with informal helpers in a client's network on a case-by-case basis. One consideration is whether the case manager believes that the informal helper can be taught to be reliable about confidentiality. Case managers may use a method known as "widening the pool of confidentiality": The case manager and client determine together, on a case-by-case basis, who should be given personal and private information as the need to share information arises (Ballew & Mink, 1999).

f. School Social Work: The NASW and the School Social Work Association of America (SSWAA, 2001) have offered the following guidelines to help school social workers evaluate the need to share confidential information about students and their families:

- A school social worker should disclose information obtained from students or parents to other school personnel on a "need-to-know" basis and only for compelling professional reasons.

- When obtaining informed consent at the beginning of services, a school social worker should inform the student and the student's family that he cannot guarantee absolute confidentiality and should explain the limits of confidentiality. These limits include his mandate to report known or suspected child abuse and to disclose information if a student indicates an intent or a plan to harm herself or others.

- A school social worker should be aware that parents have the right to inspect and review their child's education records (see also below). However, personal notes about a student kept by the social worker for his own use are not considered educational records and are, therefore, confidential.

- In a situation in which there are no clearly defined laws or policies in place to help the social worker evaluate whether to share confidential information, the social worker should consider his responsibility to the student and weigh this against his responsibility to the student's family and the school community. The social worker should consider two key questions: (a) Why is it important for this information to be shared and (b) how would the student and the student's family benefit if I decided to share the information? In weighing these questions, the social worker should remember that his actions will be judged by a reasonable standard of care criterion (i.e., what a reasonable person in a similar situation would do).

- Finally, barring an emergency that immediately threatens the life of the student or another person, the social worker should involve the student and the student's family in decisions involving a breach of confidentiality before sharing any confidential information.

School social workers must also be familiar with laws, regulations, and local policies that impact confidentiality in their practice. The **Federal Educational Rights and Privacy Act (Buckley Amendment)** applies to educational settings and grants parents (and students over the age of 18) the right to inspect their children's (their own) educational records. Therefore, parents have the right to review the contents of their minor children's school records, other than secure testing material and the social worker's personal notes. The social worker, however, should interpret all content that the parents review in language that they can understand.

g. Employee Assistance Programs (EAPs): Under ordinary circumstances, the fact that an employee has consulted with an EAP, as well as the details of that interview, and any information about an employee's condition or treatment cannot be revealed without the employee's consent. When an employee receives EAP services as the result of a referral by her employer or manager, however, the employer or manager may be given *limited* information – i.e., he or she can be told if the employee kept the appointment, whether the employee needs treatment, and whether the employee accepted treatment. The employer or manager should not be given *any* other private or confidential information about the employee without the employee's consent.

Of course, confidentiality can be breached in the context of an EAP in those same situations that it can be breached in other contexts, such as when disclosure of certain information is necessary to prevent serious, foreseeable, and imminent harm to the employee/client or another identifiable person. The therapist should inform the employee of these and all other limits to confidentiality at the beginning of services.

h. Military Settings: Normally, client confidentiality should not be breached even in military settings. Department of Defense rules and policies, however, may require breaches of confidentiality that would, in other settings, be unethical and illegal. In particular, military rules state that (a) confidentiality can be breached without a client's consent when a federal law, state law, or service regulation imposes a duty to report information; and (b) privilege can be broken to ensure the safety of military personnel and/or the accomplishment of a military mission (Dao & Frosch, 2009).

i. Past or Planned Criminal Behavior: A client's confession to a crime she committed in the past is a privileged communication, and you have an ethical obligation to keep that information confidential unless the "crime" was child abuse or (in many states) elder or dependent adult abuse. Similarly, you would not be required to disclose information about a crime that a client intends to commit in the future unless that crime meets the standards of a duty to protect/warn situation (the duty to protect/warn is discussed later in this section).

j. Spousal/Partner Abuse: As a social worker, you have NO reporting mandate in cases of spousal/partner abuse involving victims age 18 or older. You cannot disclose any confidential information about the situation without the client's permission to do so. (For information on cases in which the victim is an older adult, see the review of laws pertaining to elder abuse later in this section.)

Advising Clients of the Limits of Confidentiality

Standard 1.07 of the Code of Ethics says that you should explain to your clients and other interested parties the nature of confidentiality. That is, you should discuss with clients the limitations to their right of confidentiality. In particular, you should discuss (a) the circumstances when confidential information may be requested and (b) when disclosure of confidential information may be required by law. An example of the former is when another professional involved in your client's case requests confidential information, and an example of the latter is when you are required by law to report that a client is abusing her child. You should discuss the limits of confidentiality with a client as soon as possible in the relationship and then as needed during the course of the relationship.

Information about the limits of confidentiality is often included in an office policies form that clients read and sign at the beginning of therapy. Also, HIPAA's privacy rule requires therapists to provide clients with a written Notice of Privacy Practices at or before the beginning of treatment that indicates how protected health information will be used and disclosed.

Note that court-ordered clients often have additional limitations on their right to confidentiality (this was discussed above), and this often includes their therapist having to report to the court (and/or probation officer) when the client does not attend her therapy sessions. You must inform the client about this requirement at the beginning of treatment.

Disclosing Confidential Information With Valid Consent

The general rule is to avoid releasing confidential client information to third parties without a written authorization from the client or her legal representative. In other words, you can disclose confidential information, when appropriate, with **valid consent** from a client or from a person legally authorized to consent on behalf of a client.

You should obtain a signed **release of confidential information** (a "release") whenever a client asks you to disclose confidential information to others and whenever a client consents to your own or another person's request that confidential information be released. For example, you should obtain a signed release of information from a client in the following situations: (a) when speaking to a client's family, friends, teachers, or employers, to other professionals (e.g., physician, previous therapist, psychiatrist), or to anyone else to collect collateral information or for any other reason; (b) when referring a client to another professional or agency; (c) when communicating with a client's insurance company; and (d) when a client allows or requests you to release confidential information about her treatment for a legal proceeding. Note that under Federal law, specific and separate releases are required to disclose HIV status and/or substance abuse treatment.

The following specific guidelines are important when you are communicating with other professionals about a client:

- When you refer a client to another professional or agency, you should obtain a release from the client so that you can share necessary information and follow-up on the referral. You should also obtain a release from a client if you will need information from a referring professional.

- Even if a client has given her permission to the other professional, you still should obtain a release from the client yourself before communicating with the other professional.

- If a physician, teacher, or other professional requests a client's records from you and the client has signed an appropriate release, you should comply while keeping in mind your other obligations. For instance, you should not provide raw test data to another professional if you believe that he or she is not qualified to interpret them. In addition, you must provide only information that is relevant to the other professional's request.

- Having a friendship or other personal relationship with a professional who contacts you for information about a client does *not* relieve you of your obligation to have permission from the client before sharing confidential information with that professional or before even acknowledging that you ever saw the client for therapy or other services.

Sometimes parents or others who are paying for an adult client's treatment assume that they have a right to be given confidential information about the client, but, in fact, their involvement does not afford them this right. You should make information available to these entities *only* at the client's request or when the client has consented to have it released at the request of another and only when disclosure is in the client's best interests. At the beginning of the relationship, you should clarify with all involved persons (in this situation, the client and those paying for her treatment) the conditions surrounding the release of information.

Finally, if a client does not want you to share confidential information with other professionals involved in her case, difficult ethical problems may arise. As a social worker, you can avoid such problems if you notify a client in advance of your role and your employer's and agency's policy in regard to sharing confidential information when it is in a client's best interests to do so.

Disclosing Confidential Information Without Valid Consent

There are situations in which a social worker is required or permitted to breach confidentiality without authorization and these situations are addressed in the Code of Ethics as well as in certain laws. With regard to the Code of Ethics, Standard 1.07 states the following:

- In general, you should protect the confidentiality of all information you obtain in the course of your professional service. An exception to this occurs when there is a **compelling professional reason** to disclose the information. Specifically, the assumption that you will keep information confidential does *not* apply when (a) you need to disclose certain information to prevent serious, foreseeable, and imminent harm to a client or others, or (b) laws or regulations require you to disclose certain information without a client's consent.

- In these situations, you should disclose the least amount of confidential information necessary to achieve your intended purpose. In other words, you should disclose only information that is directly relevant to the purpose for which you are making the disclosure.

- To the extent possible, you should inform a client about the disclosure of confidential information and the possible consequences. When feasible, you should inform the client *before* you make the disclosure.

Note that the latter two requirements apply whenever you disclose confidential information based on a legal requirement or a client's consent.

1. The Client is a Danger to Self (Suicide): If you believe that a client is at risk for suicide, you must take appropriate actions to ensure the client's safety. Depending on the level of risk, your actions may include attempting to establish a safety contract with the client, contacting the client's family, or having the client hospitalized (see Section X in Interventions with Clients/Client Systems for more information). The primary issue is that you must do what you believe is necessary to protect the client from harming herself – if a breach of confidentiality is necessary to achieve that goal, it is both ethically and legally permitted.

When determining what needs to be done to protect the client, however, you should consider your options carefully. Overall, you want to protect the client from harm, while also violating her confidentiality as little as possible. For example, it may be possible, based on the client's ability and willingness to comply with a safety contract, to maintain her confidentiality. Or, it may be sufficient to contact only the client's family rather than involving emergency personnel. Or, when the risk is high, the client might be willing to follow your recommendation to enter a hospital voluntarily. However, when the client poses a serious, foreseeable, and imminent danger to herself and is unable or unwilling to comply with less intrusive protective measures, then you need to breach confidentiality to protect her. For example, you would be permitted to initiate the process to have the client placed on an involuntary hold in a hospital.

2. The Client is a Danger to Others: When a client poses a serious danger to other people but no potential victim is readily identifiable, hospitalization may be indicated, and involuntary hospitalization would necessitate a breach of confidentiality (see Section X in Interventions with Clients/Client Systems for more information).

When a potential victim *is* readily identifiable, the situation is different: You are required to take certain steps that may result in a breach of your client's confidentiality when, based on a threat you hear from the client, you believe that she poses a serious, foreseeable, and imminent danger to a readily identifiable person. The **Tarasoff case**, which is relevant to this requirement, involved a lawsuit brought by the parents of Tatiana Tarasoff, a student at the University of California's Berkeley campus, against a psychologist and psychiatrist, the University Regents, and the campus police. Ms. Tarasoff was shot and stabbed to death by her former lover, Prosenjit Podar. Mr. Podar had informed a psychologist at the University's counseling center of his intent to kill Ms. Tarasoff. Although the therapist contacted the campus police, Mr. Podar was found to be rational when he was questioned by them and was released. The psychologist did not hear from Mr. Podar again, and Ms. Tarasoff was killed a few months later. The California Supreme Court's ruling, on a rehearing of the case, included the following statement: "When a psychotherapist determines, or pursuant to the standards should determine, that his patient presents a serious danger of violence to another, he incurs an obligation to use reasonable care to protect the intended victim against such danger. The discharge of such duty, depending on the nature of the case, may call for the therapist to warn the intended victim of the danger, to notify the police, or to take whatever steps are reasonably necessary under the circumstances" (Tarasoff v. Regents of University of California, 1976, p. 426).

The Tarasoff ruling is commonly cited as establishing a "**duty to warn**." However, as shown above, the ruling actually prescribes a "**duty to protect**" an intended victim by (a) warning this person, (b) notifying the police, or (c) taking other reasonable steps.

After the ruling in the Tarasoff case, California adopted a statute that requires a therapist to make a reasonable effort to warn the potential victim and to notify the police when a client makes a serious threat of physical violence against a readily identifiable victim, and many states have followed California's lead on this, although the specific requirements vary from state to state. In states without such a law, the duty to protect/warn applies as a general principle, and many legal experts have recommended that therapists practicing in those states follow that principle.

Understanding the following points will help you in applying the "duty to protect/warn" to situations that may be presented in exam questions:

"Serious threat of physical violence": The word "serious" is left open to interpretation, but many have interpreted this to mean that the threat must be "imminent" in order for the duty to protect/warn to arise. In effect, "serious" refers to the seriousness of the client's intentions rather than to the degree of violence the client intends to inflict. Some factors to consider when determining whether a threat is serious would include the client's past history of violence and the context in which she has made the statement. Clients may make threatening statements in your presence without intending to act on them, for example, when they are discussing emotionally charged material, and such statements often do not constitute "serious" threats. If you are unclear about the meaning of a client's threat or unsure of what to do, you should immediately seek consultation with a qualified colleague and/or an attorney.

"Identifiable person/victim": The duty to protect/warn applies only when you can identify a potential victim (or victims), but this does not mean that you have to be able to name the victim. Instead, the Tarasoff decision refers to persons who are "readily identifiable" by the therapist, but not necessarily known. Thus, if a client threatened to go into a specific bar in your town and shoot randomly, the patrons in the bar would be considered identifiable victims. Or, if a client threatened to blow up a building and identified the building to you, the people who may be in the building when the client carries out her threat would be considered identifiable victims.

Situations in which the duty to protect/warn does NOT apply:

- *Someone besides the client is the dangerous party:* The duty to protect/warn exists only when the client is the potentially violent party. For example, if a client told you about someone else who intends to murder a specific individual, your duty to protect/warn would not exist. You would, however, want to encourage the client to report this threat to the police or take some other appropriate action. If you wanted to contact the police yourself, you would have to get the client's permission before doing so.

- *A third party tells you that your client has threatened to harm someone:* If a third party, such as a friend or relative of the client, tells you that your client has threatened to harm someone, you are not required to either notify the police or warn the intended victim, even if the threat is serious. You would, however, want to address the issue with the client to determine if the client does, in fact, pose a danger to another person and, if so, take appropriate action. (NOTE: Because courts have started clarifying "duty to protect" laws, the responsibility of therapists in this situation now varies from state to state; remember, however, that the ASWB exam won't test knowledge of state laws.)

- *There is no "readily identifiable" victim:* Sometimes, you may encounter a client who seems generally dangerous, but you can't identify a potential victim. The duty to protect/warn covers only situations in which there is a "reasonably identifiable victim or victims" (although, as stated above, this does not mean that you have to be able to name the victim).

3. HIV and the Duty to Protect/Warn: Whether a social worker has a duty to protect/warn when a client who is HIV positive reveals that she is sharing needles or engaging in unprotected sex with an identifiable partner remains a grey area. You have several options in this situation: (a) The initial course of action would ordinarily be to maintain the client's confidentiality and encourage the client to engage in safe-sex practices, refer the client to a support group, and discuss the possible legal consequences of engaging in unprotected sex. (b) You *may* decide to breach the client's confidentiality in order to protect the intended victim; but, before doing so, you should explain the decision to the client and attempt to get the client's consent. If the client does not consent and you breach confidentiality, you may be charged with professional misconduct and face legal action by the client. As noted by Leslie (2012), breaching confidentiality in this situation has not yet been legally tested.

Of course, consulting with a colleague and/or attorney is always good strategy to help determine the best course of action. In addition, to reduce the risk of liability, consultations, discussions with the client, and the rationale for any decisions and actions should be documented in the client's record.

Finally, people who are HIV positive are obligated to inform their sexual and/or needle-sharing partners about their serostatus and the possibility of HIV transmission, and, in some states, they may face legal consequences if they fail to inform and then infect their partner with HIV. From a clinical standpoint, it's important for you to educate clients with HIV disease about this obligation and to monitor their progress in fulfilling this duty. If a client is reluctant to inform a partner, you should actively assist the client to make the disclosure. For example, you might use role-playing exercises to help the client practice telling her partner.

4. Child Abuse Reporting: According to ethical standards, you can disclose confidential information without a client's consent when disclosure of confidential information is required by law. One important legal exception to confidentiality exists in cases of child abuse.

The **National Child Abuse Prevention and Treatment Act** (PL 93-247) was enacted by Congress in 1974 and resulted in the establishment of the National Center on Child Abuse and Neglect to assure the coordination of policies and the development of services and programs. To receive available funds, a state had to create an agency responsible for investigating maltreatment; establish a reporting system; pass laws that protect minors from mental, physical, and sexual abuse; and provide guardians ad litum to represent children's interests in court cases. Although the laws vary from state to state, all 50 states (and Washington, D.C.) now have **Child Abuse and Neglect Reporting Laws** that require social workers to make a report with an appropriate agency when, within their professional capacity, they know or have good reason to suspect that a minor is being or has been abused or neglected. These laws grant immunity from civil or criminal liability when reports have been made in good faith.

a. Basic Reporting Requirements: If the victim of child abuse is still a minor (under age 18), and you learned about the child abuse within your professional capacity, you have an obligation to file a child abuse report. This is true even if the abuse happened a while ago and/or has ended.

If you are ever faced with an ambiguous reporting situation, you should generally either file a report or call a child protective services agency for counsel.

b. Adult Reports of Childhood Abuse: An interesting dilemma may be posed when an adult client reveals to you that she was abused as a child. Child abuse and neglect reporting laws do not usually require social workers to make a report when an *adult* client discloses that she was abused before she turned age 18. You must, however, be alert to the possibility that the client's abuser may now be abusing other minors. If you have good reason to believe that the client's abuser is still victimizing minors, then you are obligated to file a report related to that current abuse. For instance, if an adult client tells you that she was abused by her father and that her father is now abusing her younger siblings who are minors, you would have to make a report to the appropriate authorities. The same thing would be true if the client's abuser was a teacher who is still teaching children.

In this situation, you can also discuss with the client the possibility of filing assault charges with the police or pursuing a civil action for damages for the abuse she suffered. This should include a discussion of the possible negative effects or outcomes of the action, and you must allow the client to make her own decision without any pressure. This approach can be useful when you believe that the client would benefit therapeutically from confronting the experience through the legal system.

c. Minors Engaging in Sexual Activity: All sexual intercourse with a female under age 18 who is not the wife of the sexual partner is unlawful sexual intercourse (statutory rape), but not all unlawful sexual intercourse is reportable as child sexual abuse. The following guidelines can help you in answering exam questions on this topic:

- Sexual activity involving a minor *under* age 14 is *always* reportable as child abuse, whether or not the sexual activity is consensual.

- If a sexual relationship includes a minor (any male or female under age 18) and that minor is being *forced* or *coerced* in any way to participate in the sexual activity, you *must* file a child abuse report. This is true even when the minor's sexual partner is also a minor.

- For *consensual* sex involving a minor, the following guidelines generally apply in most states: (a) If the minor is aged 16 or 17, you should file a report if the minor's sexual partner is at least *five* years older than the minor. (b) If the minor is aged 14 or 15, you should file a report if the minor's sexual partner is at least *three* years older than the minor.

d. Third-Party Information About Child Abuse: Even when you learn about child abuse from a third party, you must make a report if the information is revealed to you in your professional capacity. For example, if a client tells you that her adult son often hits his 2 year old when he misbehaves to the extent that the child has cuts and bruises, you are required to file a report even though you did not learn about the abuse directly from the victim or perpetrator. In contrast, if you overhear a conversation at the supermarket that leads you to believe a child is being abused, you are not legally required to make a report but may choose to do so as a private citizen.

Responding to a Subpoena

A **subpoena** is a legal document that requires the recipient to testify at a designated place and time, to provide records, or both. The individuals who may issue a subpoena depend on the type of case (civil or criminal) but include a judge, a court clerk, and the attorney for the plaintiff or defendant. There are two common types of subpoena: A *subpoena ad testificandum* orders a person to testify before the ordering authority or face punishment; and a *subpoena duces tecum* orders a person to bring physical evidence (e.g., records) before the ordering authority or face punishment.

The Code of Ethics addresses responding to a subpoena by stating that, if a legally authorized body, such as a court of law, orders you to disclose confidential or privileged information without a client's consent and you believe that such disclosure could result in harm to the client, you should ask the court to withdraw the order, try to limit the order as narrowly as possible, or keep the relevant records under seal, where they are unavailable for public inspection. "Under seal" is a procedure allowing sensitive or confidential information to be filed with a court without becoming a matter of public record. Permission for the material to remain under seal must generally come from the court.

Other guidelines for responding to a subpoena would ordinarily involve the following steps (APA, 2006):

- The first step is to determine if the subpoena is legally valid. The subpoena might not be valid, for instance, because the court is outside your jurisdiction or the subpoena was improperly served. If you are unsure about the legality of the subpoena (or have any other questions about how to respond to it), the best strategy is to seek legal advice.

- If the subpoena is valid, a response is required (e.g., you must appear in court at the time requested). However, you should first contact the client to discuss the implications of providing the requested information and obtain the client's consent to release confidential information if her consent is not attached to the subpoena: (a) If the client does *not* consent, you or your attorney can attempt to negotiate with the party who issued the subpoena. If that party continues to demand that the information be provided, you may seek guidance from the court informally through a letter or have your attorney file a motion to quash or modify the subpoena. (b) If the client *does* consent, you should release only information you believe is relevant to the case unless otherwise ordered by the court. (Note that a subpoena is still valid even when a client does not give permission for the release of confidential information. Thus, you should contact the client's attorney or your own attorney to discuss the matter or contact the attorney who issued the subpoena to request to be released from it. Unless you receive the requested release, you must appear as requested in court but should claim the privilege on the client's behalf; see below.)

- When a request for confidential information arises for the first time during testimony at a deposition or in court, you should claim the psychotherapist-patient privilege on the client's behalf and refuse to provide the information until ordered by the court to do so. Note that you should claim the privilege even if you recognize that, under the circumstances, an exception to privilege applies because it is up to the court (not you) to decide whether or not privilege is waived.

- When the court issues an order to provide testimony or produce documents and your efforts to have the order modified or vacated have been unsuccessful, you must comply with the order to avoid being held in contempt of court. However, to be consistent with ethical guidelines, you should provide only information that is relevant to the case and present subpoenaed records in a sealed envelope marked "confidential." It is illegal to destroy or tamper with records for the purpose of avoiding disclosure.

HIPAA's Privacy Rule

The **privacy rule** is one of three parts of the Health Insurance Portability and Accountability Act (HIPAA) and was designed to ensure the security of a patient's **protected health information** (**PHI**), which includes any individually identifiable health information that is transmitted or maintained in any medium and is "created or received by a health-care provider ... and relates to the past, present, or future physical or mental health or condition of an individual" (45 CFR 160.103). The privacy rule is "triggered" (must be implemented) when a provider transmits PHI electronically in connection with one of several transactions including health-care claims, health-care payment, health-care plan payment, or enrollment or disenrollment in a health plan. Once the privacy rule is triggered, it applies to all of the provider's transactions, not just those that are conducted electronically.

The privacy rule states that a written authorization from the patient is required before a provider discloses PHI *except* when the information is being disclosed for routine purposes related to treatment, payment, or health-care operations ("TPO") or in other legally defined situations (e.g., when disclosure is necessary to avert a serious threat to the health or safety of the patient or other person). The authorization must include a description of the information to be disclosed; indicate the name and function of the person/entity authorized to use the information; indicate the expiration date of the authorization; and include a statement informing the patient of her right to receive a copy of the authorization and to revoke it.

Confidentiality and Clients Who Are Minors

Minors, like adults, are legally and ethically entitled to a confidential relationship with their therapists; and, in general, therapists should protect the confidentiality of minors (even from the minors' parents when appropriate) and ensure that minor clients understand the limits of confidentiality. Additionally, NASW's Standards for the Practice of Social Work with Adolescents says that social workers must "maintain confidentiality in their relationship with youths and of the information obtained within that relationship."

1. Explain Your Policies With Regard to Confidentiality: When you are working with a minor, a good strategy is to discuss confidentiality at the beginning of therapy with the parents and the child. This discussion should take into account the needs and concerns of the parents, the best interests of the child, and the impact of breaching the child's confidentiality on the therapeutic relationship, and it should end with an agreement between all parties about what information revealed by the child will and will not be shared with the parents. If an agreement can't be reached that suits all involved parties, including you, then you can choose to refer the minor to another provider for treatment.

Generally speaking, a responsible social worker will be sensitive to the parents' concerns and give them regular reports on their minor child's progress in treatment, without revealing specific confidential information.

2. Releases of Confidential Information: As with any client, you may release or share confidential information about a minor client if you have appropriate authorization to do so. When the client is a *nonemancipated* minor and is being seen with parental consent, authorization to release confidential information must come from at least one of the minor's parents when the parents are married, from at least one divorced parent with legal custody, or from the legal guardian of the minor. A parent or legal guardian, for example, would have to give permission for you to communicate with a minor child's teacher or to examine the child's medical records. Last, minors in **foster care** are usually wards or dependents of the court. Therefore, when working with a minor who's in foster care, it is not necessary to have the biological parents or legal guardian sign releases of information for the minor, as it would be if the minor were living with them.

3. Preventing Harm: As when working with an adult client, you can disclose confidential information about a minor client without consent when such disclosure is necessary to prevent serious, foreseeable, and imminent harm to the client or another identifiable person.

4. Other Situations Involving the Confidentiality of Minors:

a. Minor's Parents Insist on Receiving Information: In some instances, the parents of a minor client may insist on receiving specific confidential information about their child's treatment; the parents may even insist that they have a legal right to the information. In this situation, you should not release the information if you feel that doing so would be detrimental to your client. If you were unable to satisfy the parents by explaining to them that releasing the information would likely harm their child or her therapy, then you could consult an attorney for advice.

b. Custody Questions: When the legal custody of a minor child is disputed or unclear, special policies concerning the noncustodial parent's right to obtain information may be necessary. You should consider the best interests of the child as well as the rights of parents. In your actual practice, you should consult your state's laws concerning the rights of noncustodial parents; state laws, however, are not the subject of ASWB exam questions.

c. Pregnancy of a Minor: You are not ethically or legally required to tell a minor's parents about the minor's pregnancy. The minor is entitled to a confidential relationship with you.

C. Client Self-Determination

Ethical Standards

Self-determination is an ethical principle that recognizes the right and need of clients to be free to make their own choices and decisions. As a social worker, your ethical responsibilities with regard to client self-determination include the following (Ethical Standard 1.02):

- You respect and promote the right of your clients to self-determination whenever it is socially and/or clinically responsible to do so.

- You help your clients determine and clarify their goals and work to improve your clients' capacity and opportunity to change and meet their own needs.

- You may limit a client's right to self-determination when, based on your professional judgment, you conclude that the client's actions or potential actions pose a "serious, foreseeable, and imminent" risk to self or others. These situations (suicidality, danger to others) were discussed in the review of Confidentiality in this section.

In addition, Standard 1.14 of the Code of Ethics says that, when you act on behalf of a client who lacks the capacity to make an informed decision, you should take reasonable steps to protect the interests and rights of this client.

Discussion

1. Respecting and Promoting Self-Determination: To behave in an ethical manner, you must respect and promote the right of your clients to self-determination whenever it is socially and/or clinically responsible to do so.

a. Establish Mutuality at the Start of the Relationship: **Mutuality** refers to mutual efforts by you and the client to work on the problem. To establish mutuality, you adopt a posture of professional competence, while, at the same time, communicating that you and the client are equal partners in the helping relationship who are both responsible for what happens in the helping process.

b. Facilitate Decision Making and Problem Solving: **Role induction** is used at the start of the relationship to prepare clients for the helping process by, among other things, clarifying the roles of the social worker and the client in this process. Your primary role is to facilitate decision making and problem solving by the client, and, to do this appropriately, you must respect the client's right to and need for self-determination, while recognizing their inherent strengths, talents, and skills in doing so. The following guidelines can help you to do this effectively:

- When helping a client explore alternatives and make decisions, you must respect the client's values and belief systems and avoid imposing your own. You don't have the right or responsibility to make decisions for your clients. A client might make a decision that you disagree with, but, because she is the one who must live with the decision, she has the right and responsibility to make it.

- You should expect a client to work toward the intervention goals and convey this expectation to her. Be willing to challenge or confront a client when she is not making reasonable progress.

- You must avoid creating dependence. For example, you should use interventions that allow a client to learn problem-solving skills and prepare and empower her to ultimately function and cope without your assistance.

- You must allow a client to participate as much as possible in decisions that affect her life and keep her informed of what you're doing on her behalf.

2. Incompetency (Incapacity): Adults are presumed to be legally competent and are entitled to make all legal decisions for themselves. Only if they are determined to be incompetent by a court can adults be deprived of their right to make their own decisions; a court will then appoint a guardian to make decisions for them.

Definitions of incompetence (also called "incapacity") vary from state to state, but they generally require the following: (a) The person must be incapacitated in some way; *and* (b) as a result of that incapacity, the person must be unable to care for herself or manage her own property. In other words, in order to establish incompetency, there must be evidence of mental or physical impairment *and* evidence of impaired adaptive behavior. Both of these criteria are necessary since, for example, a person can be mentally ill but still competent to make decisions.

State laws vary in terms of the rights retained and lost by adults who are found to be incompetent. Generally, however, an adult who is found to be incompetent loses her right to make significant decisions concerning her life. Some of these rights, including the right to consent to medical or mental health treatment, may be transferred to a **legal guardian** who serves as a decision-maker for the person. The person over whom a guardianship is imposed is called a ward. A guardian generally has the same power to make decisions for his or her ward as a parent has to make decisions for his or her child. Many states, however – including those that recognize the concept of "limited guardianship" – limit the authority of a guardian to do certain things (such as commit a ward to a mental hospital) without having a court order or express authorization.

In most states, the following people may file a petition asking a judge to appoint a guardian for an adult person: the person who needs help, the person's spouse, another relative of the person, any interested state or local entity, or any other interested person or friend. The appointed guardian may be a family member, friend, or private professional guardian. In some states, the guardian can be an organization. For people who do not have any friends or family available to act as guardian, a judge may appoint a public guardian.

Finally, **minors** are considered to be legally incompetent and unable to make legal decisions for themselves. A minor's parent(s) will make legal decisions for the minor. If the minor has no parent capable of making legal decisions or no living parent, then the court will appoint an adult to serve as a legal guardian for the minor.

D. Competence

Ethical Standards

Scope of competence is addressed in several sections the Code of Ethics.

Ethical Responsibilities to Clients – Competence (Standard 1.04)

- You should provide services only within the bounds of your education, training, license/certification, consultation received, supervised experience, or other relevant professional experience.

- You should represent yourself as competent only within the bounds of your education, training, license/certification, consultation received, supervised experience, or other relevant professional experience.

- If you wish to provide services in substantive areas that are new to you or apply intervention techniques or approaches that are new to you, you should engage in appropriate study, training, consultation, and supervision beforehand.

- You must ensure that the individuals who prepare you to use a new intervention or technique are competent in the intervention or technique.

- If there are no generally recognized standards for a new area of practice, you must safeguard the competence of your work and protect your clients from harm by (a) using careful judgment and (b) taking responsible steps, such as engaging in appropriate education, research, training, consultation, and supervision.

Ethical Responsibilities to Clients – Cultural Awareness and Social Diversity (Standard 1.05)

- You should understand culture and the role it plays in human behavior and society.

- You should recognize that strengths exist in all cultures.

- You should have knowledge about your clients' cultures.

- You should be capable of providing services that are sensitive to people's cultures and to differences among people and cultural groups.

- You should get education about and attempt to understand the nature of social diversity and oppression related to race, ethnicity, national origin, color, sex, sexual orientation, gender identity or expression, age, marital status, political belief, religion, immigration status, financial and legal status, and mental or physical ability.

Ethical Responsibilities in Practice Settings – Supervision and Consultation and Education and Training (Standards 3.01 and 3.02)

- If you provide supervision or consultation (whether in-person or remotely), you should have the necessary knowledge and skill to supervise or consult appropriately. In addition, you should provide supervision or consultation only within your areas of knowledge and competence.
- If you function as an educator, field instructor for students, or trainer, you should provide instruction only within your areas of knowledge and competence, and your instruction should be based on the most current information and knowledge available in the profession.

Ethical Responsibilities as Professionals – Competence (Standard 4.01)

- You should accept responsibility or employment only on the basis of existing competence or the intention to acquire the necessary competence.
- You should seek to become and remain proficient in your professional practice and the performance of your professional functions.
- You should critically evaluate and stay current with new knowledge related to social work.
- You should routinely review the professional literature.
- You should participate in continuing education related to social work practice and social work ethics.
- You should base your practice on recognized knowledge, including empirically based knowledge, related to social work and social work ethics.

Discussion

1. Working Within the Boundaries of Your Competence: You should consider the following factors when deciding whether you are competent to take a case:

Who are the clients? For example, a family, a couple, a parent and child, and so on. How are you qualified by education, training, and experience to work with these clients (e.g., to provide family therapy?).

Are there "differences"? For example, an elderly couple, a gay couple, an African-American family, a low-income family, and so on. As a result of these differences, will you need to seek supervision or consultation to ensure the competence of your services? According to the Code of Ethics, a "competent" social worker knows about different cultures (especially those of the clients he serves) and recognizes and understands individual differences and the role culture plays in individual behavior and society as a whole. A social worker who has never worked with clients belonging to a particular ethnic group, for example, would want to make sure that he is providing a member of that group with competent services by seeking supervision or consultation.

Sometimes the client, rather than the social worker, will have concerns about a "difference." For example, a Asian-American client meeting with a white social worker may express a strong preference for working with a therapist who is Asian-American. In this situation, the social worker would ordinarily comply with the client's request, while initially acknowledging and exploring the client's concerns, and refer her to one or more qualified Asian-American therapists. This would be true even if the social worker is competent to treat this client himself. This applies equally to other "differences" that a client believes would interfere with effective treatment (e.g., race, sexual orientation, gender).

What signs and symptoms does the client present? For example, symptoms of a possible personality disorder or psychotic disorder. Are you qualified by your education, training, and experience to treat this disorder? If not, you should refer the client to a mental health professional who is.

Is the client's problem amenable to the services you are qualified to provide? For example, does the client have complaints that may be related to a medical disorder? Will you need to refer the client to a physician for evaluation before deciding whether you should take the case? (Of course, even if it turned out that a client's symptoms were caused by a medical disorder, you could still see the client to address psychosocial problems stemming from the disorder or her efforts to cope with it, if the client wanted to do that. In this situation, you'd want to collaborate with the medical professionals who are treating the client.)

2. An Aspect of a Case Falls Outside the Boundaries of Your Competence: The Code of Ethics implies that if a needed service falls outside the boundaries of your competence, you should seek supervision or consultation or make a referral. It also states that you should arrange for appropriate consultations and referrals based principally on the best interests of your clients.

When an aspect of a case falls outside the scope of your competence, you have three options, depending on the circumstances – seek information, seek supervision or consultation, or make a referral:

Seek information: Seeking information is *not* an adequate way to compensate for a lack of competence in a particular area. However, it is possible that you would have the skill to treat a case, but in order to fully meet the client's needs, would have to obtain certain additional information. For instance, when working with a divorcing couple with children, you may need to learn more about your state's laws related to dissolution of marriage and child custody.

Seek supervision or consultation: According to ethical standards, you should seek the advice and counsel of colleagues whenever such consultation is in the best interests of a client. Seeking supervision or consultation is an appropriate option if you have the general skill to treat a case, but there is a particular aspect of the case that you have not dealt with extensively or at all. For example, if you have experience treating substance use disorders but have never worked with someone who abuses crystal meth, when presented with such a case, you would want to seek consultation with someone who has expertise in working with people who abuse crystal meth. When consultation is an adequate supplement to your existing ability to treat a case, consultation is sufficient. Otherwise, you would need to refer the client to a more qualified professional.

Make a referral: The Code of Ethics requires you to refer a client to another professional or agency whenever that professional's specialized knowledge or expertise is needed to fully serve the client. For instance, there may be aspects of a case that are outside the legal scope of social work practice. As a social worker, for example, you cannot prescribe medication for a client. Thus, you would have to refer a client who may need to take psychoactive medication to a psychiatrist for a medication evaluation. In this situation, although the client requires specialized services from another professional, you wouldn't have to let go of her case: You would refer the client to the psychiatrist for the medication evaluation and possible prescription, and assuming you are competent to do so, would continue providing the client with other services she needs (e.g., counseling, case management).

Choosing consultation vs. referral: If, for example, you have experience in treating specific phobias and wish to treat a client who has agoraphobia, then it would probably be adequate for you to seek consultation. However, if you use psychodynamic techniques in your practice and believe that a client would benefit most from behavioral techniques, then consultation would not be sufficient. Instead, you would need to refer that client to a professional who has expertise in using behavioral techniques.

3. Incompetence of Colleagues: The Code of Ethics also addresses the issue of a colleague's incompetence (Standard 2.09): (a) When you have direct knowledge of a social work colleague's incompetence, you should consult with that colleague, if feasible, and help the colleague take remedial action. (b) When you believe that a social work colleague is incompetent *and* the colleague has not taken adequate steps to address the incompetence, you should take action through appropriate channels developed by your employer, the agency, the NASW, a licensing or regulatory body, and other professional organizations.

4. Impaired Therapists: Social workers are ethically obligated to take appropriate action whenever personal problems or other factors might interfere with their ability to provide effective professional services. The Code of Ethics (Standard 4.05) says the following:

- You should not allow your personal problems, psychological distress, legal problems, substance abuse, or mental health difficulties to interfere with your professional performance and judgment or to threaten the best interests of persons for whom you have a professional responsibility.

- If your personal problems, psychological distress, legal problems, substance abuse, or mental health difficulties interfere with your professional performance and judgment, you should (a) immediately seek consultation and (b) take appropriate remedial action by getting professional help, adjusting your workload, terminating your practice, or taking any other steps necessary to protect your clients and others.

The Code of Ethics also requires you to take action to address a *colleague's* impairment (Standard 2.08): (a) When you acquire direct knowledge of a social work colleague's impairment due to personal problems, psychological distress, substance abuse, or mental health difficulties, and the impairment is interfering with the colleague's practice effectiveness, you should consult with that colleague, if feasible, and help him take remedial action. (b) When you believe that a social work colleague's impairment is interfering with his practice effectiveness *and* that the colleague has not taken adequate steps to address the impairment, you should take action through appropriate channels developed by your employer, the agency, the NASW, a licensing or regulatory body, and other professional organizations.

E. Informed Consent

Ethical Standards

The Code of Ethics (Standard 1.03) says the following with regard to informed consent:

- You should provide your services to clients only within the context of a professional relationship.

- You must obtain a valid informed consent from a client in order to provide your services, ideally in writing. At minimum, you should document in the client's record that informed consent was provided.

- As part of obtaining an informed consent, you must tell a client about the purpose of your services, the risks related to these services, the limits to these services due to a third-party payer's requirements, relevant costs, reasonable alternatives, the client's right to refuse or withdraw consent, and the time-frame covered by the consent.

- When informing a client about the matters mentioned above, you must use clear and understandable language and give the client an opportunity to ask questions.

- If a client is illiterate or has difficulty understanding the primary language used in your practice setting, you should take steps to ensure that the client obtains as much understanding as possible about the available services. For example, you can provide the client with a detailed verbal explanation. If possible, you should bring in a qualified interpreter or translator.

- If a client lacks the capacity to provide informed consent, you must attempt to protect the client's interests. You should take reasonable steps to increase such a client's ability to give informed consent for herself: You should (a) provide the client with an explanation of the services to the extent possible, based on her ability to understand the information; (b) seek to obtain consent from an appropriate third party; and (c) take steps to ensure that the third party acts in a manner consistent with the client's wishes and interests.

- If a client is receiving your services involuntarily, you should inform the client about the nature and extent of the services and her right to refuse the services.

- If you provide services via electronic media (e.g., computer, telephone, radio, TV), you should notify those who receive your services in this manner of the risks and limitations associated with these services.

- You should get a client's informed consent (ideally in writing) before audiotaping or videotaping the client.

- You must get a client's informed consent before allowing a third party to observe therapy sessions or other services provided to the client.

Discussion

Informed consent refers to the right of a client to be given adequate information about the treatment process and procedures before making the decision to participate in treatment. This includes information about the risks, limitations and benefits of treatment, the client's rights and responsibilities, and the limits of confidentiality.

1. Necessary Conditions for Informed Consent: Legally, the following three conditions must be met for consent to be truly informed:

Capacity: The client must have the capacity to make rational decisions about therapy. A client under the influence of alcohol or drugs or who is experiencing an acute psychotic episode does not currently have the mental capacity to consent to treatment. So, for example, if a client presents for therapy while under the influence of drugs, you should wait to obtain consent until after the client is sober.

Minors are considered to lack the capacity to provide informed consent. When a client is a minor, you would obtain informed consent from at least one of the minor's parents or the legal guardian. Similarly, if a client has intellectual disability or otherwise lacks the mental capacity to give informed consent, you should determine if the client has a legal guardian or someone acting under a legal power of attorney who can provide informed consent on the client's behalf. If there is no legal guardian, you should decline to provide treatment until one is appointed. In addition, when a client lacks the capacity to provide informed consent, you should notify the client about the general nature of the proposed treatment in a manner consistent with the client's ability to understand, seek the client's assent, and consider the client's preferences when making decisions that affect her.

Comprehension: The client must be given adequate information and understand the information sufficiently to make an informed decision. This means that information about therapy must be presented in understandable language and that the client must have an opportunity to ask and receive answers to her questions.

If a client is illiterate or has difficulty understanding the primary language used in your practice setting, you should take steps to ensure that the client obtains as much understanding as possible about the available services. For example, you can provide the client with a detailed verbal explanation or bring in a qualified interpreter or translator.

Voluntariness: The client must give her consent freely (without coercion). Voluntariness may be an issue when, for example, a client comes for treatment at the request or urging of a family member or other person. Obtaining informed consent from such a client may require you to explore and address the client's negative feelings about coming to therapy. This may be necessary in order to ensure that the client's consent is truly voluntary.

Finally, an informed consent should be appropriately documented. The method of documentation is, in most cases, up to the social worker, but many authorities recommend obtaining a formal signed, written consent.

2. Informed Consent and Mandated Services: Even when your services are court ordered or otherwise mandated, you still should inform the client of the nature of the anticipated services, including the fact that the services are court ordered or mandated and all limits to confidentiality, before proceeding. For example, in court-ordered therapy, there are limits to confidentiality that are set by the court (e.g., the court often wants to know that the client attended therapy and may want some general content), and clients should be informed of these limits at the start of therapy.

3. Child Custody/Guardianship Questions: The issue of consent to treatment can be complicated in cases involving children whose parents are divorced, and one parent has full custody or, alternatively, the parents have joint custody. In these situations, should consent be obtained from one parent (e.g., the parent who has full custody) or from both parents? The best course of action is to check your state's laws and determine what arrangement was agreed upon by the parents. For the sake of the ASWB exam, the general rule would be to obtain the consent of the parent with legal custody before providing services to a child; or, in cases of joint legal custody, to make an attempt to get consents from both parents.

In some cases, a minor will have a **legal guardian** who has been appointed by a court to take care of the minor and her property. A minor child's court-appointed guardian has the right to request and consent to treatment for the child. Approval from the court or from the child's biological parents is not necessary.

Minors in **foster care** are in the custody of the child welfare agency and are wards or dependents of the court. Therefore, when working with a minor in foster care, it is not necessary to get consent for treatment from the minor's biological parents or legal guardian: When a minor is a ward or dependent of the court, this means that the court has taken over responsibility for the minor's care, and, therefore, consent for treatment comes from the court.

4. Emancipated Minors: Emancipation is a procedure by which minors become legally responsible for themselves, and their parents are no longer responsible, financially or otherwise, for them. While the laws regarding the emancipation of minors vary from state to state, emancipated minors are generally freed from parental custody and control and essentially become "adults" in many ways. This means, among other things, that emancipated minors can consent for themselves to medical, dental, and mental health treatment.

5. HIPAA's Notice of Privacy Practices: The Notice of Privacy Practices (NPP) is a new consent form required under HIPAA's privacy rule. You must give the NPP to clients at the beginning of or prior to the first session. You also must provide copies of the NPP to clients when they request them. Even if you already give clients a pre-HIPAA office policies and informed consent form, you still must provide them with the NPP. You also should continue to give clients your pre-HIPAA office policies and informed consent form as it details other issues about which clients should be informed. (Additional information on HIPAA is provided later in this section.)

6. Research Practices: When participating in research, the social worker must follow the protocol for the protection of human rights. You must obtain a client's (or client's guardian) written informed consent to participate in a research study or project. You should include the following in writing: (a) purpose of the study, and (b) activities to be accepted by the client should the client agree to participate. The social worker should discuss with the client the right to withdraw from the research study at any time without disruption of any social work services.

F. Payment for Services

Ethical Standards

The Code of Ethics (Standard 1.13) says the following with regard to payment for services:

- When setting a fee for your services, you should make sure that it is fair, reasonable, and consistent with the services you perform.

- When setting a fee for your services, you should give consideration to a client's ability to pay.

- Ordinarily, you should avoid accepting goods or services from your clients as payment for professional services. Such "bartering" arrangements, especially those involving your services, may result in conflicts of interest, exploitation, and inappropriate boundaries in your relationship with a client.

- In very limited circumstances, you can explore and may engage in bartering with a client – i.e., you may do so when you can demonstrate that the bartering arrangement is an accepted practice among professionals in your community, is viewed as essential for the provision of services, has been negotiated without coercion, and has been entered into at the request of the client and with the client's informed consent. If you accept goods or services from a client as payment for your professional services, you bear the full burden of demonstrating that this arrangement will not harm the client or the professional relationship.

- You should not ask for a private fee or other remuneration when providing services to a client who is entitled to such available services through your employer or agency.

Discussion

1. Setting Your Fee: While a social worker employed in an agency uses the fee structure of his employing agency, a social worker in independent practice must establish a fee structure. A social worker's fee must be fair, reasonable, and consistent with the services he performs, and he should give due consideration to a client's ability to pay. The following guidelines are also important:

- You may charge a fixed fee (which may be reduced in certain situations) or use a sliding fee scale. Sliding fee scales are not addressed in the Code of Ethics but are generally considered acceptable as long as they are fair and serve the best interests of clients.

- You should never let the fact that a client does or does not have insurance influence the determination of your fee: You should have either a fixed fee or a policy which you use to determine the fee for each client (e.g., a sliding fee scale based on a client's ability to pay). Your fee or fee policy should not be altered on the basis of a client's insurance coverage or lack thereof. You may not legally reduce/waive insurance co-pays without approval from the insurance provider.

- Providing **pro bono (free) services** is recommended by the Code of Ethics but not required. For example, you might choose to provide free services to a client who cannot afford to pay you at all. Free sessions, however, should never be used in advertising media as enticements to draw new clients into your practice.

Finally, social workers sometimes need to raise the fee they charge their clients, for example, because the costs of providing their services have increased. Before deciding to raise a client's fee, you must consider the client's financial status and treatment needs. An alternative is to raise your fee for new clients, while maintaining old clients at your previous rate.

2. Avoiding Exploitation: You must avoid exploiting clients and others through your financial arrangements. It would be unethical to treat a low-income client until her insurance runs out and then refer her to a low-cost community clinic (a practice known as "creaming and dumping").

It would also be unethical to withhold services to pressure a client to pay her bill. For instance, you should not abruptly terminate services to a client or refuse to supply another professional with a client's records simply because the client owes you money. (See Termination of Services in this section for more information on this.)

3. Clients in Short-Term Financial Crisis: If a client can no longer afford to pay for your services, the best course of action would be to continue providing therapy at a mutually agreed-upon reduced fee. If this is not possible, you might schedule fewer appointments, postpone therapy for an agreed-upon period, see the client for free while she is in the midst of the financial crisis, or help the client locate other services. An *unacceptable* option in this situation is abandoning the client. Be aware that even referral of the client to a lower-cost provider *may* constitute abandonment if you and the client have developed a working relationship and treatment is well underway.

Last, in an emergency situation, you would have an obligation to continue providing treatment to the client, regardless of her ability to pay, until the crisis has been resolved.

4. Unpaid Fees: To behave in an ethical manner, you should adhere to the following guidelines if you need to collect unpaid fees from a client:

- You should first discuss the matter of unpaid fees with the client. Similar to when a client is in a short-term financial crisis, you and the client may be able to reach an agreement that accommodates the client's financial situation. When a client says that she cannot pay the debt or refuses to pay it, consider simply forgiving the debt.

- You have no ethical duty to continue treating a client who does not pay for services in the manner that has been agreed upon and may terminate treatment in an appropriate manner (see Interruption or Termination of Services in this section).

- You can use a collection agency but only after notifying the client of your intention to do so and giving the client an opportunity to pay the fees that are owed within a specified period of time. In addition, you should notify clients of your policy regarding the use of collection agencies as part of the informed consent process at the beginning of treatment. And, when a collection agency is used, you must give the agency only essential information, such as the client's name and address and the amount owed. You must not disclose anything about the content of your work with the client.

- To avoid the use of outside services, you might consider calling a client to ask her for payment; however, in doing so, you must be aware of the ethical and legal considerations. Ethically, there may be problems with confidentiality if you call the client at home or work. Legally, consumer protection laws protect people from harassment regarding bills, and you may get into legal trouble if your calls are perceived by the client as being too coarse or zealous.

5. Barter: Bartering is not completely prohibited by the Code of Ethics. However, before accepting a bartering arrangement, a social worker should consider possible alternatives (e.g., offering the client services at low or no cost or referring the client to another therapist who provides free or low cost services), as well as the potential consequences of barter. For example, the exchange of certain services for therapy – e.g., housekeeping or childcare – would be clearly unacceptable because of the potential negative effects on the therapeutic relationship if the client does not perform those services satisfactorily (Canter et al., 1994).

6. Referral Fees: The Code of Ethics prohibits social workers from accepting or paying referral fees. Ethical Standard 1.16(c) says you should never give or receive payment for a referral when no professional service is rendered by the referring social worker. Note, however, that referral fees are fees that are paid simply for the referral (i.e., they do not represent the actual costs of making the referral). For example, if a social worker refers clients to a colleague and allows the colleague to use his office to see those clients, it would be acceptable for the social worker to charge a fee that represents the costs associated with the colleague's use of the office space.

7. Insurance Fraud: Insurance fraud is both unethical and illegal. Acts that constitute insurance fraud include (a) routinely waiving copayments without informing the insurance company; (b) assigning an inaccurate diagnosis in order to be paid by the insurance company; (c) billing for a missed appointment without making it clear that the appointment was missed; (d) filing a claim for individual therapy when couples or family therapy was provided; (e) providing couples therapy and billing both parties' insurance companies for individual therapy; (f) having someone else sign an insurance claim; and (g) providing services that are not deemed medically necessary or services which over a period of time are no longer benefiting the client (Griswold, 2010).

G. Conflicts of Interest and Dual/Multiple Relationships

Ethical Standards

The Code of Ethics (Standard 1.06) says the following with regard to conflicts of interest and dual or multiple relationships:

- You should be alert to and avoid conflicts of interest that interfere with your exercise of professional discretion and objective judgment.

- You should inform your clients when a real or potential conflict of interest arises.

- If such a conflict arises or is likely to arise, you should take reasonable steps to resolve the conflict in a way that considers the clients' interests first and protects their interests to the greatest extent possible.

- Sometimes, in order to protect a client's interests when there is conflict of interest, you will need to terminate the professional relationship. If you must terminate a professional relationship due to a conflict of interest, you must provide for proper referral of the client.

- You should not take unfair advantage of any professional relationship you have or exploit anyone to further your own personal, religious, political, or business interests.
- You should not engage in dual or multiple relationships with a client or former client when there is a risk of exploitation or potential harm to the client.
- If a dual or multiple relationship is unavoidable, you should take steps to protect the client. In this situation, you are responsible for setting clear, appropriate, and culturally sensitive boundaries.
- You should avoid communication with clients using technology (such as social networking sites, online chat, e-mail, text messages, telephone, and video) for personal or non-work-related purposes.
- When providing services to two or more people who have a relationship with each other (e.g., couples, family members), you should clarify with all parties which individuals you will view as the "client," and the nature of your professional responsibilities to each person receiving your services.
- If you anticipate a conflict of interest among the individuals receiving your services or anticipate having to perform in potentially conflicting roles (e.g., you may be asked to testify in a child custody dispute or the clients may initiate a divorce proceeding), you should clarify your role with all of the individuals involved. If this type of conflict of interest arises, you should take appropriate steps to minimize it.

Discussion: Conflicts of Interest

Difficulties can arise in family or couples therapy when the goals of different family members or the partners are diametrically opposed (e.g., in couples therapy, the husband may be hoping to improve the marriage, while the wife wants to get a divorce). The ethical standards relating to conflicts of interests are designed, in part, to help you avoid such difficulties: As noted above, whenever you provide services to two or more people who have a relationship with each other (e.g., couples, families), you should clarify with all parties which individuals you will view as the "client" and the nature of your professional responsibilities to each person receiving your services.

Who is considered the "client" can vary, depending on the nature of the treatment and the social worker's philosophy. Often, in family or couples therapy, the family or couple is considered the "client," and, in many cases, a social worker will not also see one member of a client-family/couple for ongoing individual therapy. One of the primary reasons for this is that doing so can create clinical and ethical difficulties (e.g., problems related to confidentiality, the potential that issues that should be addressed with the family or couple will be addressed primarily in individual therapy, perceptions by one of the clients that the social worker favors the other partner or is colluding with him or her).

Discussion: Dual/Multiple Relationships

Dual or **multiple relationships** occur when social workers assume two ("dual") or more ("multiple") roles at the same time or sequentially with a client. An example is providing therapy to an employee, friend, or relative. Note that a dual relationship is a separate and distinct relationship, which means that the second relationship is not clearly related to the therapeutic relationship. For example, seeing a client in both individual and family therapy does not constitute a dual relationship but providing therapy to a current employee does. When a dual relationship exists, there is a risk that the client or former client will be exploited, primarily because of the power differential that is a basic part of the therapeutic relationship.

The Code of Ethics says the following with regard to dual or multiple relationships (Standard 1.06): (c) You should not engage in dual or multiple relationships with a client or former client when there is a risk of exploitation or potential harm to the client; and if a dual or multiple relationship is unavoidable, you should take steps to protect the client and are responsible for setting clear, appropriate, and culturally sensitive boundaries.

1. Nonsexual Dual Relationships: Nonsexual dual relationships include an additional relationship with the client (or former client) and, in some circumstances, a relationship with a client's spouse, partner, or family member. Examples of unacceptable nonsexual dual relationships include borrowing money from a client, improper exchange of gifts with a client, developing a close personal relationship with a client or a client's family member, going into business with a current client or her spouse, and accepting a family member or close friend of one's own as a therapy client. With regard to **gifts**, accepting a small gift from a client does not usually violate ethical obligations, but even in this case, a therapist would want to consider the client's motives for giving the gift before accepting it (Koocher & Keith-Spiegel, 2008).

2. When a Nonsexual Dual Relationship is Unavoidable: The ethical prohibition against dual and multiple relationships is not absolute, in part, because a dual or multiple relationship may be unavoidable in some situations. In a rural or small community, for example, a social worker is likely to encounter his clients and former clients in contexts other than the treatment setting. As long as the social worker is sensitive to the potential harmful effects of dual or multiple relationships, these encounters are not likely to be viewed as a breach of ethical standards.

When a dual or multiple relationship is unavoidable, you must take appropriate steps to protect the client or former client and assume full responsibility for setting clear, appropriate, and culturally sensitive boundaries. With regard to chance encounters with clients, for example, Knapp and VandeCreek (2003) suggest that therapists establish a "you first" policy that allows the client to decide if she will acknowledge you outside the service setting. When faced with a more complex situation – for instance, you live in a very small town and discover that you and a client attend the same church – it's a good idea to seek supervision or consultation so that you can discuss with someone objective the appropriate alternatives available to you.

As implied above, you must also consider the **cultural context**. Among clients from some cultures (e.g., Hispanic), behaviors such as inviting their social worker to share a meal or attend a family function and gift-giving are not usually signs of dependency or a lack of appropriate boundaries. Attending a family function in this situation may be important for building trust and rapport.

3. Sexual Relationships: The Code of Ethics says the following with regard to sexual relationships (Standard 1.09):

- You should never, under *any* circumstances, engage in sexual activity, inappropriate sexual communications through the use of technology or in person, or sexual contact with a current client. This prohibition applies whether sexual contact with a current client is consensual or forced.

- You should not engage in sexual contact with a client's relatives or other people with whom the client has a close personal relationship when there is a risk of exploitation or harm to the client. Sexual activity or sexual contact with these individuals can harm the client and make it difficult for you and the client to maintain appropriate professional boundaries. You bear the full burden for setting clear, appropriate, and culturally sensitive boundaries.

- You should not engage in sexual activity or sexual contact with a former client because doing so may harm the client.

- If you become sexually involved with a former client, or want to claim that there is exception to the ethical standards because of unusual circumstances, you bear the full burden of proving that the former client has not been exploited, coerced, or manipulated, either intentionally or unintentionally.

- You should not provide clinical services to anyone with whom you have had a prior sexual relationship because doing so has the potential of harming this person and is likely to make it difficult for you and this person to maintain appropriate professional boundaries.

H. Clients' Access to Their Records

Ethical Standards

The Code of Ethics (Standard 1.08) says the following with regard to access to records:

- You should provide your clients with reasonable access to records concerning them.

- If you are concerned that such access will result in misunderstanding or serious harm to the client, you should provide the client with help in interpreting the records and consult with the client about the records.

- You should limit a client's access to her records, or part of the records, only in exceptional circumstances, as when there is compelling evidence that seeing certain information in the record would result in serious harm to the client.

- If you limit a client's access to all or part of her records, you should document in the client's file her request for the records, and the reasons why you withheld all or part of the records from her.

- When providing clients with access to their records, you should take steps to protect the confidentiality of other people identified or discussed in the records.

Discussion

The ownership of records and other data is governed by law. The client owns the contents of the record, and the social worker (or the organization where a social worker works) owns the physical document. Laws relating to confidentiality, privilege, and mandatory reporting determine how this ownership is exercised, however: Unless otherwise directed by statute or a court order, you can only do with a record what the client authorizes you to do.

Although clients have the right to review and obtain information from their records, they do not have the right to all of the material contained in them. For example, clients would ordinarily not have the right to see your informal notes about them or information transmitted in confidence to you by another person. In addition, ethical standards indicate that, when a client requests to see her records, you can withhold certain information contained in the record if you have compelling evidence that seeing that information would seriously harm the client.

Finally, the exact requirements regarding client access to their records also depend on state laws and on the context. You should be familiar with the state laws that apply to your practice, but state laws will not be asked about on an ASWB exam. As far as federal law, **HIPAA** stipulates that patients must be permitted to review and amend their medical records. Under HIPAA, you may deny a client access to her records *only* if access is reasonably likely to endanger the life or physical safety of the client or another person; or if the information in the record makes reference to another person (unless that person is a health care provider) and access is likely to cause substantial harm to the other person.

I. Client Transfer: Potential Client Receiving Services From a Colleague

Ethical Standards

If a potential client is receiving services from another provider or agency, you should proceed with caution. The overriding consideration is the client's well-being. The Code of Ethics (Standard 3.06) says the following with regard to client transfer:

- If a potential client who is receiving services from another agency or colleague contacts you for services, you should carefully consider the client's needs before agreeing to provide your services.

- To minimize possible conflict and confusion, you should discuss with the potential client the nature of her current relationship with the other service provider, and the implications, including possible risks or benefits, of entering into a professional relationship with you.

- If a new client has been served by another agency or colleague, you should discuss with the client whether consultation with the previous service provider is in the client's best interest.

Discussion

The primary considerations when a prospective client is receiving services from another mental health professional are the client's welfare and the reason why the client is seeking mental health services from more than one provider. You are not prohibited from seeing clients who are receiving services from another mental health professional, but you would never want to duplicate the services of another provider for an extended period of time. Insurance providers typically will not pay for any duplication of services.

When a client is seeing the other professional for a *different* problem than the one she wants to work on with you, it's likely to be acceptable for you to provide your services to the client. For example, if a client is seeing a behavioral therapist to help her quit smoking and then contacts you to deal with marital problems, it would be acceptable for both you and the other therapist to see the client in therapy. The same would be true if the client were seeing the other therapist with her spouse for couples work and wanted to see you for individual therapy. You'd simply need to get the client's permission to consult and/or collaborate with the other professional to define your different goals and contributions to treatment.

In contrast, when the client is seeing another mental health professional for the *same* problem she wants to work on with you, the best course of action would be to explain your ethical responsibilities to the client and determine why the client is seeking the same services from two different providers. If you determine that there is no benefit for the client in seeing two providers, then you should decline to provide your services. Note that it is acceptable to see a client once under such circumstances for evaluation and consultation. In fact, you often do not know before the first session that a client is seeing another therapist (or "shopping"). Therefore, it is a good practice to have a question on an intake form about previous experience with mental health services.

Finally, clients often become dissatisfied with counseling or therapy at the very point when it is beginning to work. Therefore, if a client reported dissatisfaction with another provider as the reason for coming to see you, issues such as resistance would have to be sorted out from "incompetent other therapist." Then depending on the source of the client's dissatisfaction, it might be useful to send the client back to the other provider to discuss the problem thoroughly before she makes a decision to terminate and begin working with you.

J. Interruption or Termination of Services

Ethical Standards

The Code of Ethics (Standards 1.15 and 1.17) says the following with regard to interruption or termination of services:

- You should terminate your services to a client and your professional relationship with the client when your services and the relationship are no longer needed or no longer serve the client's needs or interests.

- You should take reasonable steps to avoid abandoning a client who still needs your services.

- You should withdraw your services abruptly only under extraordinary circumstances, giving due consideration to all aspects of the situation and taking care to minimize possible negative effects.

- If you must terminate your services to a client abruptly, you should, when necessary, assist in making appropriate arrangements for alternative services for the client.

- If you work in a fee-for-service setting, you may terminate your services to a client who is not paying her overdue balance if the following conditions are met: (a) the financial contractual arrangements have been made clear to the client, (b) the client is not an imminent danger to self or others, and (c) you have addressed and discussed the clinical and other consequences of nonpayment with the client.

- You should not terminate your services to a client for the purposes of pursuing a social, financial, or sexual relationship with the client.

- If you anticipate the termination or interruption of your services to a client, you should inform the client promptly, and seek the transfer, referral, or continuation of services, in accordance with the client's needs and preferences.

- If you are leaving an employment setting, you should tell your clients about appropriate options for the continuation of services, and the risks and benefits associated with their options.

Discussion

Based on these standards, you should begin the process of formally ending your relationship with a client when the treatment goals have been achieved. That is, it is unethical to continue treating a client after the client has met her treatment goals and, therefore, no longer needs your services. Additionally, you should discuss the termination of your services with a client when it is clear that the client is not benefiting from your services. When termination is necessary before the treatment process is completed, you must make appropriate referral to other helping sources. For more information on termination of services, see Section IX in Interventions with Clients/Client Systems.

K. Representing and Advertising Your Services

The following are some of your ethical responsibilities regarding representing, advertising, or publicizing your services (Ethical Standards 4.06 and 4.07):

- Social workers are prohibited from misleading clients, the public at large, colleagues, and employers about their background, skills, and areas of expertise. They must make sure that all representations to clients, agencies, and the public of their professional qualifications, credentials, education, competence, affiliations, and services and of the results to be achieved are accurate. For example, it would be misleading to clients and potential clients for a social worker to include "Ph.D." on a business card if his doctorate has no connection to his qualifications, education, or competence as a social worker (e.g., his Ph.D. is in American history).

- Offering guarantees of help or improvement to potential clients in brochures or other advertisements is unethical.

- Using **client testimonials** is not prohibited. However, you *are* prohibited from soliciting testimonial endorsements from current clients (or other people) who, because of their particular circumstances, are vulnerable to undue influence. You are also prohibited from soliciting from such vulnerable individuals their consent to use their prior statements as testimonial endorsements.

- Social workers should not seek to publicize their own work in the media. For example, the Code of Ethics urges social workers to provide appropriate professional services in public emergencies to the greatest extent possible and to place service to others above their own self-interests. In this situation, then, a social worker who provides professional services in a local emergency should not seek public recognition of his efforts through the media.

L. Other Professional Issues

HIPAA

The Health Insurance Portability and Accountability Act (HIPAA, P.L. 104-191) began to be implemented in 2003. A key goal of HIPAA regulations is to control the rising costs of health care by simplifying and standardizing the insurance claim process. HIPAA's Title I was intended to protect health insurance coverage for workers and their families when workers change or lose their jobs. HIPAA's Title II, the Administrative Simplification provisions, is designed to improve efficiency and effectiveness in the health care system. Title II addresses the privacy, security, and electronic transmission of health information and requires the Department of Health and Human Services (DHHS) to establish national standards for electronic health care transactions and national identifiers for providers, health plans, and employers.

1. Key Terms Associated With HIPAA: Familiarity with the following terms will help you understand HIPAA requirements:

Covered entity (CE): A covered entity (CE) is a health care provider who transmits health information in electronic form in connection with a HIPAA transaction. HIPAA rules regulate CEs.

Protected health information (PHI): PHI is also known as medical information, health information, health care information, medical records (e.g., confidential medical-psychotherapy records). PHI includes any information that identifies the individual or that could reasonably be used to identify the individual.

Privacy rule: HIPAA's privacy rule applies to PHI. The privacy rule is designed to provide greater protection for health information by requiring certain policies, procedures, and business arrangements to control access to and use of PHI. Because state confidentiality laws are generally more restrictive than HIPAA regulations, they preempt many aspects of HIPAA's privacy rule with regard to PHI; this means that by following state laws and professional regulations with regard to confidentiality, you are already in compliance with many aspects of HIPAA's privacy rule.

Security rule: HIPAA's security rule also protects PHI, but it focuses on the physical aspect of your office/agency such as issues of access to your files and computers.

Transaction rule: HIPAA's transaction rule requires standard formatting of electronic transactions such as health care claims and inquiries about plan eligibility and coverage. It also covers "standard code sets."

"Use" and "disclosure": Under the privacy rule, "use" means the sharing, employment, application, utilization, examination, or analysis of individually identifiable health information (PHI) by an entity that maintains such information. For psychotherapists, for example, "use" means using PHI to provide psychotherapy. "Disclosure" means the release, transfer, giving access to, or disclosing of PHI to an outside entity.

Need-to-know requirement: The need-to-know requirement requires that access to PHI by staff in an office/agency be assigned on a need-to-know basis (access to only the information needed to do their jobs).

Minimum-necessary requirement: The need-to-know requirement described above applies to people who already have access to PHI, such as the staff in an agency. The minimum-necessary requirement addresses the amount of PHI that can be disclosed to *outside entities*: (a) HIPAA regulations require you to restrict the disclosure of PHI to the minimum amount of information needed and to apply policies and procedures to ensure that the minimum amount of information is disclosed in response to requests from outside entities (e.g., collection agencies, insurance claim forms). (b) Because the minimum-necessary requirement is open to interpretation, you must be careful when deciding how much to disclose. Note, however, that the minimum-necessary requirement is similar to ethical requirements governing confidentiality. For example, under both HIPAA and the Code of Ethics, you should never give clinical information to a collection agency. You should also be cautious when disclosing information to family members, unless they are clients in family therapy or the client has given prior authorization. (c) Finally, this requirement does not apply to disclosures you make in response to a client's signed authorization – the authorization itself should specify clearly what information can be released.

Privacy officer: HIPAA regulations require the designation of a privacy official by each covered entity to be responsible for "the development and implementation of the policies and procedures" necessary for compliance.

TPO: TPO stands for treatment, payment, and health care operations. HIPAA defines TPO as follows: (a) "Treatment" includes providing psychotherapy treatment, consultation with other health care providers, and referral of a client from one provider to another. (b) "Payment" includes activities you undertake to receive reimbursement for providing professional services to a client, such as billing, determining eligibility, claims management, collection activities, or obtaining payment under a reinsurance contract, review of health care services for medical necessity, coverage, and appropriateness or utilization review activities. (c) "Health care operations" include quality assessment, underwriting, reviewing the competence or qualifications of health care professionals, premium rating, medical review, legal services, auditing and business management, and general administrative activities.

2. HIPAA's Privacy Rule: HIPAA's privacy rule is designed to provide increased protection for protected health information (PHI) and requires covered entities (CEs) to implement procedures to assure their clients' privacy.

a. Privacy Rule Requirements: The privacy rule requires CEs to (a) inform clients of privacy policies and how they are implemented; (b) secure clients' records; (c) obtain a client's authorization for sharing information for nonroutine purposes, such as marketing; (d) inform business associates of privacy practices; and (e) train employees so that they understand privacy procedures.

b. The Notice of Privacy Practices (NPP): The **Notice of Privacy Practices** (**NPP**) is a consent form required under HIPAA's privacy rule that helps clients understand how their PHI is used and disclosed. You must give the NPP to clients at the beginning of or before the first session. Even if it is otherwise permitted, you are prohibited from using or disclosing information in a way that is not described in the NPP.

Key contents of the NPP include the following: (a) a description and at least one example of the types of uses and disclosures you are permitted to make for TPO; (b) a statement that the client has the right to revoke her consent in writing; (c) a description of each of the other (non-TPO) purposes for which you are permitted or required to use or disclose PHI without written consent or authorization (e.g., mandatory reports such as child abuse reports, duty to protect/warn); (d) a statement that other uses and disclosures will be made only with the client's written authorization and that the client may revoke her authorization; (e) a statement of the client's right to request restrictions, receive confidential communications, request amendments, receive an accounting of disclosures, and obtain a paper copy of the NPP on request; (f) a description of your legal duties; and (g) instructions on filing complaints with you or the DHHS. The NPP should also include a written acknowledgment from the client (e.g., "I acknowledge the receipt of this notice").

Finally, in emergency situations, the NPP must be provided as soon as reasonably feasible; you don't have to obtain an acknowledgment in emergency situations.

3. HIPAA's Security Rule: HIPAA's security rule is designed to provide a minimum standard of protection of protected health information (PHI) stored or transmitted electronically.

a. Security Rule Requirements: The security rule covers the physical security of confidential information including such issues as access to office files, computers, phones, e-mails, and faxes. The security rule applies to all confidential information about clients. It requires agencies, clinics, etc., as well as therapists in private practice to make an assessment of all potential threats to the security of PHI (e.g., unauthorized people accessing computer files, computer viruses). Based on this risk analysis, measures to protect the security of PHI must then be developed, implemented, and maintained. Both the risk analysis and the security plan must be documented.

b. Who Must Follow the Security Rule: HIPAA's security regulations apply to private practice therapists, agencies, clinics, etc., who electronically transmit and/or electronically maintain health information about a client. Therefore, even if a social worker in private practice doesn't transmit electronic insurance claims, he must comply with the security regulations if he maintains electronic health information about clients.

Laws Related to Elder Abuse

1. Adult Protective Services Laws: All 50 states have enacted legislation authorizing the provision of adult protective services (APS) in cases of elder abuse. APS laws establish a system for the reporting and investigation of elder abuse and the provision of social services to help the victim and address the abuse. In many states, these laws apply to abused adults who have a disability, impairment, or vulnerability as defined by state law, not just to older individuals. Some state APS laws only apply to adults who live in the community (what is called "domestic abuse"), while other APS laws also include adults who live in long-term care facilities (known as "institutional abuse").

2. Elder Protective Services Laws: Some states in the U.S. have passed separate elder protective services laws that require social workers to make a report to an appropriate agency when they learn that an elder client has been abused or neglected. These laws vary widely from state to state regarding the age at or circumstances under which a victim is eligible to receive protective services; the definition of abuse; the types of abuse, neglect, and exploitation that are covered; classification of the abuse as criminal or civil; reporting requirements (mandatory vs. voluntary); and investigation responsibility and procedures (Stiegel & Klem, 2005).

3. Long-Term Care Ombudsman Program: All 50 states have laws authorizing the Long-Term Care Ombudsman Program (LTCOP), which is responsible for advocating on behalf of residents of long-term care facilities who experience abuse, violations of their rights, or other difficulties. The LTCOP is mandated in each state as a condition of receiving federal funds under the Older Americans Act. If an LTCOP discovers elder abuse or neglect when responding to complaints about a facility, a referral is made to an APS program or the agency responsible for investigating institutional abuse, to the agency responsible for licensing and certifying the facility, or to a law enforcement agency. In some states, the LTCOP fulfills the APS function and has the legal authority to investigate and respond to abuse occurring in long-term care facilities.

4. Other Laws: As noted, some states have laws that provide criminal penalties for certain forms of elder abuse and some APS laws include a provision stating that elder abuse can be prosecuted criminally. Even when there is not a specific law authorizing criminal prosecution for elder abuse, a state's other criminal laws covering such crimes as assault, battery, rape, theft, and fraud can be used to prosecute an individual who has abused an older person. Other state laws that may apply in cases of elder abuse include those addressing guardianship or conservatorship (see Section XIV in Interventions with Clients/Client Systems), general or durable powers of attorney, and domestic violence or family violence prevention. For example, a state's domestic violence or family violence law may provide remedies such as restraining orders in cases involving elder physical abuse committed by a spouse or certain other individuals included in the state's law.

The Rights of Inpatients

1. A List of Inpatient Rights: Many states have laws that provide a bill of rights for inpatients. Inpatients usually have the right to the following (NASW, 1987):

- To receive considerate and respectful care.

- To receive information about their condition or diagnosis and participate in treatment planning.

- To give informed consent when they are mentally and physically able to.

- To refuse treatment or involvement in a research study.

- To be free from unnecessary restraints, seclusion, and physical and mental abuse. (Patients are protected from the "unnecessary use" of restraints and seclusion; however, their use is allowed if they are employed in conformity with good medical practice – that is, they have therapeutic benefit – and there is a written order from a physician or a verbal order in the patient's record that is later signed by the physician. Corporal punishment is always prohibited.)

- To know the policies and rules of the care facility and its fees.

- To have information about their personal life and treatment kept confidential.

- To communicate with and have visits from whomever they wish.

- To receive treatment in privacy.

- To not be forced to perform a service for the facility.

- To wear their own clothing.

As noted above, commitment to an inpatient facility, whether voluntary or involuntary, does *not* automatically take away a person's **right to refuse treatment**. In fact, many states have laws that restrict the use of treatments with negative side-effects, such as psychoactive drugs and electroshock therapy, and make them subject to acceptance by the patient. However, with *involuntary* psychiatric hospital patients, a lack of capacity for making an informed choice is assumed (at least for the time being), and, thus, treatment facilities are generally authorized to give medications and certain other treatments to these patients without the patient's consent when such procedures are consistent with good medical practice and there is a careful balancing of the patient's interest with those to be furthered by administering the treatment (e.g., Rennie v. Klein, 1981; Kulak v. City of New York, 1996). This is true unless specific laws or regulations require consent for special therapies. Even when consent for treatment is not required, however, a physician should consult with the patient and her family and consider their views about treatment alternatives. Minors do not usually have the right to either consent to or refuse treatment, but there are exceptions to this that differ from state to state.

In addition, involuntarily committed patients must not be denied their "**due process of law**." The Fifth and Fourteenth Amendments to the Constitution provide that no one may be deprived of "life, liberty, or property" without "due process of law." This generally means that all government actions depriving individuals of protectable interests must be reasonable and fundamentally fair, or have a constitutionally acceptable justification ("substantive due process"); and that governments must use reasonable and fundamentally fair procedures before depriving individuals of a protectable interest ("procedural due process").

Services available to help inpatients understand their rights and take action when their rights have been violated include patient representatives, patient advocates, and ombudspersons.

2. A Social Worker's Roles and Duties: The principle of client self-determination is significant in all of these roles.

> *Defining inpatients' needed rights and implementing existing rights:* This role includes acting as a patient or family advocate or representative; as an administrator who interprets policies, treatment alternatives, and procedures to inpatients and their families; or as a member of an admissions team when Medicare will pay for services or a committee who makes decisions about patient care. The social worker must know how to facilitate communication between a patient, the patient's family, and the health or mental health care facility where the patient is being treated. The social worker may be called on to provide **psychosocial data** for treatment decision making, to communicate a patient's wishes when she is unable do to so, or to meet with a mentally competent patient who is refusing needed treatment.
>
> *Education and outreach:* A social worker should engage in public education and outreach to help others understand ethical patient care and inpatients' rights.

Quality Assurance and Peer Review

1. Quality Assurance: "Quality assurance" refers to procedures and measures taken by an organization to determine whether its services or products measure up to the written standards and policies established for them.

Quality assurance programs in social work seek to determine and demonstrate that social workers meet the standards established for them. To achieve this, reviewers identify the standards of care, evaluate cases to determine if these standards are met, make recommendations for improvements, and do a follow-up review to see if improvements were achieved. These programs are usually more concerned with compliance than outcome.

For social workers, quality assurance measures include adequate education from accredited schools of social work, entry-level work experience under qualified supervision, licensing and certification, competency exams, and continuing education requirements. For the social work profession, quality assurance measures include a Code of Ethics that is available to the public, peer review, utilization review, program evaluations, professional sanctions, malpractice suits, and criminal negligence charges.

2. Peer Review: Peer review is "a formal evaluation by a specific group of one's fellow professionals to determine general competence or specific actions" (Barker, 2003, p. 320) (i.e., professional standards of intervention have been specified, and practices then are monitored periodically by one's colleagues). Peer review is frequently used for the purpose of quality assurance.

A **peer review organization** (PRO) is a formal group consisting of individuals who are members of a specific profession. These individuals meet to evaluate the work of other members of their profession, especially to evaluate how the professional has performed or achieved a specific set of tasks or objectives. The evaluation is usually done by reviewing the case records to determine if the treatment plan, methods, and outcome are consistent with the client's needs and the agency's objectives.

3. Other Related Bodies: Other groups that meet to evaluate a professional's competence and/or specific actions include committees on inquiry and ethics committees. **NASW Ethics Committee** is a group of professionals and others who meet to determine if a colleague has committed wrong-doing or been the victim of another's wrong-doing. These committees often deal with alleged violations of the Code of Ethics, violations of the law, and disputes among professionals or between professionals and clients. These committees may be sponsored by professional associations (for example, the NASW), third-party organizations, or consumers. **Ethics committees** are formal groups established by agencies and other organizations to provide professionals with opportunities to consult with one another about ethical concerns.

Liability in Partnerships and Group Practices

Social workers in private practice may form partnerships with one or more other providers in which they own and operate a practice together. When a **general partnership** is formed, each partner has "joint and several liability" for the obligations of the partnership, each partner's malpractice, and the negligent acts of all representatives of the partnership (e.g., agents, employees, staff members). Thus, one partner in a general partnership could be held personally liable for another partner's misconduct.

In a **limited liability partnership**, by contrast, the partners avoid personal liability for each other's negligent acts (and for the negligent acts of others representing the partnership). In a limited liability partnership, partner A could be held liable for partner B's misconduct only if he were directly involved in it and/or had knowledge of it while is was occurring.

The most common type of group practice is the group practice without walls (GPWW) in which several practices (from solo providers to larger practices) form a group with each individual usually maintaining his practice independence. There is joint liability in any GPWW.

(NOTE: "Negligence" is defined as a failure to exercise reasonable care or caution, resulting in someone either being harmed or being exposed to an unnecessary risk of harm. Negligence also refers to a failure to fulfill a duty necessary to protect or help another person. A professional may be guilty of contributory negligence if his failure to exercise reasonable caution, along with the negligence of another person, results in harm to a third person. Criminal, or culpable, negligence may be found if a professional has been so careless or indifferent to the safety of others that injury or death has resulted.)

Telemental Health Services (E-, Internet, Cyber Therapy, Internet Counseling)

Methods of providing online therapy (**telemental health services**) include structured e-mail exchanges, "chat" sessions in which real-time information is exchanged via the computer keyboard, more recently, live real-time two way video therapy, group "chat" sessions that are moderated by a social worker, or electronic social networks. Telemental health may be used to provide psychoeducation and supportive services to relatively high functioning individuals. Online therapy is not appropriate for high-risk individuals, or those in crisis. One reason for these restrictions is that an e-therapist lacks adequate access to the client's nonverbal behaviors. Another reason is that electronic counseling has not been subjected to appropriate scientific research to determine its efficacy as a primary or sole modality for individuals experiencing mental disorders. Social workers providing telemental health services shall take all necessary measures to ensure compliance with relevant practice standards. You need to be vigilant about the information that is included in technological communications, and ensure they are familiar with the organizational policies and/or state laws regarding use of technology, electronic communications, and social media with clients and the public.

Social workers who offer services online must meet certain accepted practice standards, including the following (Gingerich, 2002):

- Describe clearly and completely what your services consist of and do not consist of.
- Fully and accurately disclose your professional credentials and experience.
- Fully inform clients about how online services work, the skills they will need in order to use your online services, and what the possible risks are, including breaches of confidentiality.
- Request the client to provide her name and contact information in case of an emergency. (This is the recommended best practice but a person receiving e-therapy can, from a legal stand
- State your fee structure clearly (see also below).
- Deliver services exactly as you advertise.
- Make sure you have made provisions to ensure the confidentiality and privacy of your online communications.
- Maintain records of the services you provide according to professional and state-mandated standards.

In addition, NASW's Code of Ethics (Standard 1.03e) states, "Social workers should discuss with clients the social workers' policies concerning the use of technology in the provision of professional services"

With regard to fees, e-therapists should clearly state the amount of their fee on their Web page and also communicate with clients about the fee before providing their services. In terms of the fee charged, many e-therapists charge their basic hourly fee and charge for the time they spend reading and responding to each e-mail. If an e-therapist accepts credit cards, he must allow payment through a secure server or provide a telephone or fax number for the client to call with her credit card information (a therapist should *never* ask a client to send credit card information by e-mail, or in any nonsecure Web form). An e-therapist may alternatively ask client to pay by mail, via a check or money order.

Finally, the National Association of Social Workers and Association of Social Work Boards Standards for Technology and Social Work Practice ("Technology Standards") provide guidance for the use of technology in social work practice. The following are among the issues addressed by this document: (a) advocating for technology access by clients with special needs or limited access; (b) appropriate matching of online methods, skills, and techniques to the cultural and ethnic characteristics of clients; (c) development of security policies and procedures; (d) accurate marketing practices and verification of client identity; and (e) compliance with relevant laws and regulations in all states where services are provided (i.e., online practice may be subject to regulation in both the jurisdiction in which the client receives services and the jurisdiction in which the social worker provides services).

II. Social Worker Roles in Interventions with Clients/Client Systems

1. Social Worker Roles in Interventions with Clients: The roles undertaken by social workers involved in practice include the following:

Advocate: As an advocate, you work with and on behalf of clients to ensure that they receive the services and benefits to which they are entitled and that the services are delivered in ways that protect their dignity.

Broker: As a broker, you link clients with resources they need. To perform this role effectively, you need to be familiar with community resources and their eligibility criteria.

Case manager: As a case manager, you identify, plan, access, coordinate, and monitor all of the services your client needs from various providers. Clients needing case management services usually have multiple problems that require assistance from more than one provider and special difficulty in seeking help and using help effectively.

Consultant: As a consultant, you provide information and advice to individuals, agencies, institutions, etc., based on your specialized knowledge of or experience in a particular problem area, client population, or practice method.

Counselor/psychotherapist: As a counselor or psychotherapist, you help clients achieve psychological and interpersonal change and maintain their existing capacities and strengths. In performing this role, you apply your knowledge and understanding of human behavior and how the social environment affects it, assess your clients' needs and functioning, make judgments about what interventions to use, apply intervention techniques, and guide your clients through the change process (Sheafor & Horejsi, 2003).

Educator: As an educator, you provide information and teach skills to clients. For example, you teach parenting skills, educate a client about her disorder, teach strategies for dealing with anxiety, model problem-solving techniques, and teach communication or conflict resolution skills to a couple, family, or group.

Enabler: As an enabler, you create the conditions and environment in which change can occur for your clients. For example, you convey hope and encouragement, you offer suggestions and advice, you break goals into more manageable objectives, you keep your client focused on the goals of the intervention. With a couple, family, or group, you direct communications in sessions in order to resolve communication difficulties.

Mediator: As a mediator, you settle disputes between conflicting parties and restore communication between them – e.g., disputes between a client and a provider, between a client and her landlord, or between members of a family (divorce, child custody, responsibility for care of elderly parents, etc.).

Researcher/evaluator: As a researcher/evaluator, you monitor the progress of your clients, evaluate the outcome of your work, make judgments about the utility of an intervention, and/or critically review the clinical research literature.

2. Social Worker Roles in Macro (Indirect) Practice: According to Kirst-Ashman and Hull (2006), the roles social workers undertake when involved in macro practice include the following:

Advocate: As an advocate, you intervene on behalf of a macro client system to secure needed resources that are currently unavailable or to change policies or regulations that negatively affect the client system.

Analyst/evaluator: As an analyst or evaluator, you evaluate the effectiveness of an intervention, program, or agency.

Broker: As a broker, you link a system (e.g., a target population, community, or organization) to community resources and services (e.g., psychological, health-oriented, financial, legal, educational, recreational).

Educator: As an educator, you give information and teach skills.

Enabler: As an enabler, you provide support, encouragement, and suggestions to the members of a macro client system to help them complete tasks or solve problems more effectively.

Facilitator: As a facilitator, you bring people together to promote needed change by improving communication, helping to direct their efforts and resources, and linking them with information and expert assistance.

General manager/administrator: As a manager or administrator, you assume administrative responsibility for a social agency or other organizational system. "Management" encompasses all of the tasks and activities involved in directing an organization or one of its units.

Initiator: As an initiator, you start a macro change process by calling attention to a problem, need, or situation that can be improved in a community or organization. Some change efforts are undertaken to prevent a future problem or improve an existing service.

Integrator/coordinator: As an integrator or coordinator, you bring together people involved in various systems and organize their activities (e.g., you may develop and implement service linkages).

Mediator: As a mediator, you help factions (subsystems) within a community or organization resolve their differences or disagreements. You stay neutral, try to understand the positions of both parties, help the parties clarify their respective positions, etc.

Mobilizer: As a mobilizer, you identify and bring together community members and resources and make them responsive to unmet community needs. The goal may be to match resources to needs in the community, make services more accessible to residents who need them, or initiate and develop services to meet needs that previously have been unmet. This role applies in communities only.

Negotiator: As a negotiator, you act as an intermediary who attempts to settle disputes and/or resolve disagreements between various parties. You take the side of one of the parties (i.e., the macro client system) and seek to resolve the conflict on behalf of that party.

3. The Roles a Social Worker May Take in Court: Whenever you appear in court in your professional capacity as a social worker, any testimony you give must be clear, accurate, based on facts, and expressed in language that a nonprofessional can understand.

A social worker's roles in court may include the following:

Expert witness: In this role, the social worker presents a professional opinion about a situation in which he is not directly involved. Afterwards, the social worker's testimony is used by decision-makers to help them examine the evidence or consider the merits of the issue at hand. Social workers are often asked to testify as expert witnesses in disputes over child custody, child neglect, welfare rights, marital dissolution, landlord-tenant controversies, and care for people with mental or physical disabilities.

Client advocate: In this role, the social worker is a witness on behalf of his client; that is, he explains the client's social, emotional, and/or psychological problem and offers suggestions about services that the client needs.

Petitioner: This role is common in cases involving child abuse or neglect. For example, a social worker who works in child welfare may petition a court, recommending the removal of an abused child from her home under the supervision of the child welfare agency. Or, if the parents of an abused child in foster care have not cooperated with the court-ordered reunification plan, the worker may petition the court for the termination of parental rights (TPR).

Colleague: In this role, the social worker assists the court in fact-finding or supervision or by taking a mediator role, as when the case involves a divorce.

Finally, a social worker may also prepare a client to testify in court, for example, by using role-playing exercises.

III. The Social Worker-Client Relationship – Professional Use of Self

A. Conditions for Effective Helping Relationships

1. Core Conditions of Effective Relationships: The key characteristics – or core conditions – of effective therapeutic relationships are empathy, positive regard, personal warmth, and genuineness.

a. Empathy: **Empathy** involves "perceiving, experiencing, and responding to the emotional state and ideas of another person" (Barker, 2003, p. 141). When using empathy, you listen closely and respectfully in order to gain an understanding of the client and her situation. In doing so, you attempt to perceive both the manifest (surface) and latent (underlying) content of the client's messages. Your goal is to acquire and then communicate to the client an accurate understanding of her experience, from her point of view. The techniques of active listening, such as paraphrasing and reflection, are critical to your display of empathy.

b. Positive Regard: **Positive regard** involves (a) believing that all clients are people of value who are capable of positive change; (b) treating all clients with respect regardless of their appearance, behavior, life circumstances, or reason for becoming a client; (c) avoiding judgmental attitudes toward clients; and (d) avoiding either condoning or criticizing a client's thoughts and behaviors.

Displaying positive regard for clients does not mean that you must approve of or accept their negative or destructive behaviors. Rather, you need to be able to discuss these behaviors in an objective way with a client and describe how they are impacting the client and other people.

c. Personal Warmth: Conveying **personal warmth** involves responding to clients in ways that make them feel accepted and safe and that come off as sincere. Warmth is mostly conveyed nonverbally (e.g., a soft and soothing voice, a relaxed but interested posture, appropriate eye contact, smiles, gestures that convey acceptance and openness).

d. Genuineness: **Genuineness** (authenticity) is conveyed by (a) being open, nondefensive, and spontaneous; (b) matching your words and your actions; and (c) making statements that are consistent with your thoughts and feelings. The latter two skills are also known as being **congruent**. To be nondefensive, for example, you must take responsibility for your feelings (i.e., avoid blaming a client for them) and be willing to admit when you have made a mistake. In turn, these behaviors provide the client with a model for relating authentically with you and others.

Anything you reveal to a client about your own thoughts or feelings should be true, but genuineness does not require you to reveal all of your thoughts or feelings to a client. Instead, you must be sensitive to your client's needs and feelings. If you have negative feelings toward a client's behavior, consider carefully how to handle these in an ethical and therapeutic way so that you avoid damaging the relationship or harming the client. Generally, you will share your feelings with a client only when doing so is likely to increase her comfort or promote her growth in some way. You should never be hostile or abrasive with a client (even if the feeling is authentic) and must avoid emphasizing your own feelings or experiences over the client's.

Similarly, being genuine does not require you to take sides in a client's conflicts with others, even if you agree with the client's position. You should not take sides in a client's conflicts with others as doing so is likely to harm your relationship with the client, regardless of which side you have taken.

2. Professional Objectivity: Your ability to maintain your professional objectivity is critical for developing and sustaining relationships with clients that allow them to exercise their need for and right to self-determination. As a social worker, you should develop your own self-awareness and self-discipline and must be unbiased and open to other people's points of view, whether or not you agree with them. In addition, you should always bear in mind that a therapist's decision-making concerning his clients includes a subjective component, which is referred to as **clinical judgment**. It's very important to be aware of how any biases you may have can influence your clinical judgment because, for good or bad, clinical judgment influences the areas you choose to pursue or ignore when collecting data, the way you integrate and interpret the data, and the recommendations you make concerning services and resources for your clients.

Key guidelines for maintaining professional objectivity include the following:

- Never allow your own biases or personal needs to influence your decision-making concerning a client. Personal or cultural biases can enter the helping process from many different sources including your initial impressions of a client, the types of questions you ask, your theoretical perspective, your areas of interest, your cultural background, your mood, and your professional and personal experiences. Such biases may operate either consciously or unconsciously to diminish your objectivity.

- To the extent that you can, you should discuss openly with a client your own and the client's beliefs and values (including those derived from your cultures) when they may affect your understanding of the client or her situation. The spiritual domain may also affect what takes place between you and the client. For instance, if you and the client come from different spiritual backgrounds, certain words and behaviors may have different meanings.

- Although your goal is to understand your client's experience, you must remain separate from a client in order to maintain your objectivity. Moreover, if you sympathize (feel for) rather than empathize (feel with) with the client, then the client may not appreciate the need to explore her own feelings and behaviors.

- Although you must never discriminate against a client or potential client, you also must be able to recognize when you lack objectivity and, therefore, may not be qualified to provide effective services to a particular client. If you believe that your biases are likely to prevent you from serving a client's needs and interests, a referral to another qualified provider is appropriate.

- If countertransference or a similar problem emerges during your work with a client, you should seek supervision or consultation *before* the problem begins to diminish your objectivity or effectiveness or otherwise harm the client.

- When working with multiple clients, you should be alert to and avoid conflicts of interest that may interfere with your objectivity or discretion. If a real or potential conflict of interest arises, you must inform the clients and take reasonable steps to resolve it in a way that considers the clients' interests first and protects them to the greatest extent possible.

B. Responding to Client Behavior That May Impede Acceptance

Acceptance is critical to the development and maintenance of an effective helping relationship with a client. Therefore, you must monitor your reactions to client behaviors that may interfere with your ability to accept the client and should develop ways of responding that protect the relationship (Hepworth et al., 2006; Sheafor & Horejsi, 2003).

1. Defensive Communications and Behavior:

a. Understanding Clients' Defensive Maneuvers: A client may use defense mechanisms or other defensive strategies to avoid meaningful interaction or communication with you. A client who is involuntary and/or who feels angry, fearful, or threatened is especially likely to do so. Examples of defensive maneuvers a client may use include rationalization, denial, blaming others, avoidance, helplessness, labeling others, and distraction. A client may also use her physical appearance or aggressive language or behavior as a way of keeping you (and other people) at a distance. Understanding the following can make it easier to accept clients who use defensive strategies during their interviews with you:

- Defensiveness is a means of protecting oneself from real or imagined danger. Clients seeking services from social workers, for example, may fear losing control over their lives or feel afraid that they won't receive the help they want.

- A client's defensiveness may be limited to only certain situations (such as meeting with you) or be a long-term pattern. Patterns of defensiveness typically develop in response to pain or fear. For the client, such a pattern has probably served a purpose in the past by protecting her from feelings about painful life experiences or frightening events. When you feel the urge to *avoid* a client, her defensive pattern may serve to protect her from other people's interference in her life; when you feel the urge to *protect* a client or feel sorry for her, her defensive pattern (e.g., helpless behavior) may serve to help her avoid responsibilities that frighten her.

- It can be difficult for people to give up their defensive patterns because, over time, the patterns become habits of thought and behavior. If a client has frequently used denial in the past, for example, you can expect her to use denial again any time she experiences anxiety or conflict. Moreover, people are especially likely to hang on to their defenses when they are feeling anxious.

b. Responding to Clients' Defensiveness: The following strategies are useful for reducing a client's defensiveness and creating an atmosphere in which the client will feel safe acknowledging and addressing the pain and unmet needs that underlie her behavior:

- Rather than responding to the defensive behavior itself, focus on identifying what is causing the client to feel threatened and try to remove that cause.

- Emphasize active listening and efforts to help the client verbalize her feelings (don't pressure her to do this, however).

- Acknowledge situational factors that may be causing the client to feel threatened, uncomfortable, or embarrassed (e.g., say, "I know it can be embarrassing to have to ask for financial assistance").

- When the client uses a defensive tone of voice or assumes a defensive posture, respond with the opposite (e.g., use a soft tone of voice and adopt an open, nondefensive posture). If the pace of the client's speech accelerates because she's feeling angry or anxious, respond to her in a calm and comforting manner. Doing so will usually have a calming effect on the client.

- Respond to the client's *nondefensive* behaviors in ways that reinforce them. For example, use mirroring. **Mirroring** generally involves speaking at a client's pace and in a way that matches her nonverbal behavior. In this context, then, you would follow a client's *nondefensive* communications with verbal and nonverbal behavior that mirrors (imitates) hers.

- According to principles of neurolinguistic programming (NLP), your ability to communicate effectively with clients is influenced by your ability to ascertain and then work with their preferred sensory mode – visual, auditory, or kinesthetic. To respond to a client's defensiveness, identify her dominant mode of receiving information and then, to the extent that you can, use words and phrases that match it. (See Section IV in Interventions with Clients/Client Systems for more information on NLP.)

- To the extent possible, provide the client with opportunities to make choices and stay in control of what's happening in her life. Use words that convey choice, cooperation, and respect, such as "we," "it will be your decision."

Finally, you should be aware of behaviors on your part that may serve to increase a client's defensiveness. These include failing to identify yourself and your role clearly, being insensitive to the client's feelings, making judgmental statements, using jargon, quoting agency rules and policy without explaining them, appearing rushed, calling an adult by her first name without permission, being authoritarian, and being late or creating other unnecessary or unexplained delays for the client.

2. Manipulative Behavior and Lying: It can be difficult to remain objective with clients who are manipulative, especially ones who know how to "work the system" (i.e., ones who can correctly predict how you or your agency will respond under certain circumstances). The following guidelines are useful when dealing with clients who manipulate you or others or engage in deception:

- Recognize that manipulation is a coping strategy. A client may use manipulation because it works better than anything else she knows how to do. In addition, in some areas of society, being able to "work the system" is a sign of competence. It is helpful to acknowledge that the client may be trying to get their needs met and may not know any other strategies to do so.

- From the start of the relationship, be explicit in outlining your role, what you can and cannot do as a professional person, and your expectations of the client, and then be firm about adhering to these conditions. Remember that a "habitual manipulator" is always behaving in ways that help her gain control of others (e.g., she may disclose information only as it suits her purposes; slant her version of events to make herself a victim; say or do whatever she thinks is necessary to gain your sympathy or convince you of her point of view; or intimidate, threaten, or ridicule you). It is critical that you set the conditions of your work with such a client and remain firm. Do not be permissive or allow a habitually manipulative client to control things.

- If the client tries to prolong an interview by making a shocking or otherwise important disclosure at the end of the interview, inform her that you can't discuss the issue that day because the allotted time is up, but that you and she will discuss it in your next meeting. (This does not apply if the disclosure appears to involve something that places the client or someone else at risk.)

- Hold the client responsible for her behavior and don't rescue her from the natural consequences of her choices. She may need to experience these consequences before deciding to change her behavior.

- Although you must accept clients who manipulate you or others, you should not excuse or ignore this behavior. Instead, it is appropriate for you to confront manipulative behavior in a direct and authentic way (i.e., you may tell a client the feelings her behavior elicits in you). This response demonstrates that the client is important enough that you will not allow her to continue engaging in behavior that undermines her relationships.

- If you think you are being drawn into manipulation, seek consultation so that you can examine your actions and feelings with someone more objective. If you are part of a treatment team, share your concerns with team members. You may find that the client is saying very different things to other team members (she may be playing the team members against one another).

- Tell the client directly that you don't want her to lie. If you suspect that the client may be tempted to lie about a particular topic, engage her in several minutes of small talk before addressing that topic. Obvious changes in the client's voice, facial expressions, or other body language will help you detect deception.

3. Angry or Aggressive Behavior: You should be straightforward and nondefensive when responding to a client's anger or aggressive behavior. Key guidelines for dealing with a client who is angry or behaves aggressively include those listed below:

- You can avoid having a defensive reaction by recognizing that, even though the client has expressed her anger at you, it probably stems from other sources.

- Explore and attempt to resolve the client's angry feelings so that they don't damage your relationship. Use active listening and empathic responding to help the client express her feelings. When the client is calmer, identify what caused her to feel angry and try to remove that cause, if possible.

- If the client uses obscene or abusive language, remain calm and don't respond in ways that might reinforce the behavior (e.g., shock, attention). Respond immediately with verbal and nonverbal reinforcement to any part of her communication that is appropriate and constructive.

- If a client is repeatedly aggressive, respond authentically to this by describing the effects of her behavior on you (e.g., use an I-statement). This can be a new and growth-producing experience for the client because others have probably responded defensively to her aggression.

- If a client persists in verbal attacks, you may use a technique known as **fogging**, in which you offer no resistance to the client and avoid responding with either anger or defensiveness. You also calmly acknowledge to the client that she may have legitimate reasons for her anger and criticism of you (e.g., perhaps her perceptions of the situation are correct). When the client sees that her verbal attacks have no impact on you, she may abandon them.

- In the intervention phase of helping, you can assist the client to explore and learn ways of modifying her aggressive behavior and expressing her feelings in more appropriate ways that are not self-defeating.

Additional guidelines for responding to angry or aggressive behavior can be found in Section X of Interventions with Clients/Client Systems with the review of assessment procedures for clients who may pose a danger to others.

4. Helpless and Overly Dependent Behavior: Some clients prefer or insist that you tell them what to do. This type of behavior can cause you to underestimate the client's strengths and problem-solving potential. It may also lead you to create greater dependency by assuming all responsibility for resolving the client's problems. Instead, you should do the following:

- Stimulate hope and build the client's motivation. Emphasize her strengths and communicate the expectation that she is capable of responsible and autonomous behavior.
- Convey your understanding of the feelings (e.g., desperation) that underlie the behavior.
- Clarify and reinforce the mutual problem-solving nature of the helping process.
- Encourage the client to participate in developing tasks that will help her develop problem-solving skills.

5. Self-Effacing Behaviors and Statements: Individuals who repeatedly engage in self-effacing behaviors or make self-deprecating statements often feel worthless or inadequate. With such a client, you should promote and reinforce her strengths and problem-solving potential, communicate respect, and work to cultivate self-assertive behavior by empathizing with the feelings that underlie her self-effacing behavior. In the intervention, you should assist the client to become aware of this pattern, its repetitive nature, and its effects on her and others. Your objective is to help the client take steps to change the behavior and learn more assertive ways of behaving with others.

C. Demonstrating Your Authenticity

Self-Disclosure

An important skill for demonstrating your authenticity is appropriate self-disclosure (a.k.a. authentic responding). The helping skill of **self-disclosure** refers to statements you make to a client that reveal some of your own thoughts, feelings, or life experiences.

1. Guidelines for Appropriate Self-Disclosure: When used properly, the skill of self-disclosure helps a client feel more comfortable with you and can make it easier for her to talk about sensitive topics. Conversely, the improper use of self-disclosure during any phase of intervention can cause a client to question your emotional stability and professional competence and even lead her to feel manipulated. Important guidelines for using the skill of self-disclosure include the following:

- As a general rule, you should avoid self-disclosure in the early stages of a helping relationship. On the other hand, you may use a low to moderate level of self-disclosure early in the relationship if you believe that doing so would be effective for reducing a client's defensiveness.

- Normally, you would not self-disclose until rapport has developed, and the client has indicated a readiness to interact with you on a more personal level. Cultural issues are also significant, since people from some cultures may be uncomfortable relating to a social worker on a personal level.

- Self-disclosure during any phase of intervention should be limited to statements that are likely to support the treatment goals and objectives. You should self-disclose only when doing so is likely to increase the client's comfort or promote her growth in some way.

- The information you reveal should always have a clear connection to the client's concerns.

- Because your primary focus should be the client's needs, after self-disclosing, you should immediately shift the attention back to the client.

2. Reasons for Self-Initiated Self-Disclosure: You will sometimes self-disclose because a client has elicited personal information from you (this will be discussed below). In other instances, however, you may initiate authentic responding yourself as a means of achieving therapeutic goals and/or promoting the client's comfort or growth. Self-initiated self-disclosure can take the form of giving a client positive feedback, revealing your feelings, sharing information about a life experience, or offering insights or reactions related to a client's problem.

a. Providing Positive Feedback: For example, you may describe a client's positive characteristics or point out evidence of her progress. These statements often serve to increase a client's motivation and expectation that she will achieve her goals. Moreover, when you praise a client for performing a desired behavior (provide positive reinforcement), it can have the therapeutic effect of leading her to continue performing the behavior. This, in turn, can increase the client's sense of personal control. Additionally, appropriate positive feedback given consistently over time can improve the self-image of a client with low self-esteem.

b. Expressing Your Feelings: You may express positive or negative feelings to a client, but, as noted earlier in this section, you should *never* be hostile or abrasive with a client (even if the feeling is authentic) and must avoid emphasizing your own feelings over the client's.

One situation in which you might reveal negative feelings to a client is when she has put you on the spot or her behavior is unreasonable or upsetting. When using this skill, you should combine your authentic response (e.g., an I-statement) with an empathic one – this is necessary to help defuse feelings of the client that might underlie her behavior and encourage rational thought and discourse about the situation.

You may also choose to reveal your feelings when, for some reason, you experience a sense of discomfort during a session and believe that it needs to be addressed. In this situation, you would want to first think privately about your discomfort and try to identify what has caused it (for example, perhaps the client said that you seem too busy to care about her). With the client in a subsequent session, you can describe the statement or behavior that caused you to feel uncomfortable and explore the thoughts and feelings of the client that underlie the statement or behavior, using empathic responses to support the client as you do so.

c. Describing a Personal Experience: You should do this only rarely and should time the disclosure carefully. Any experience you share must be relevant to an immediate concern expressed by the client and related to the purpose of the interview. You should talk about yourself only when doing so is likely to support the treatment goals.

d. Offering Insights, Ideas, and Reactions Related to the Problem: This form of self-disclosure can have a number of beneficial effects, including increasing a client's awareness of factors that play a role in her problem, providing a client with a new perspective, helping a client understand the purposes of her feelings and behaviors, and making a client more aware of how she affects others.

3. Answering Clients' Personal Questions: If a client asks you a personal question (e.g., about your marital status, age, or values), you may share personal information if you wish to do so and/or if you determine that it would be useful to do so given the client's cultural background (e.g., if, given the client's cultural background, answering the question would be likely to facilitate the development of rapport). Before doing so, it is often useful to explore briefly their reason for asking such a question as it may reveal an unstated concern (e.g., if you do not have children, how can you help me with my out of control child). You should answer the question directly, objectively, and without emotion, and avoid focusing attention on yourself. Never share more than is comfortable for you. If a client asks about your values or attitudes, respond as honestly as possible while also communicating your acceptance of the client as a person. This is important because the client's values or attitudes may be different from yours.

If you are uncomfortable answering a personal question, you can decline to do so but should authentically share your reasons why. After rapport has developed, it can be beneficial to explore and empathize with the client's underlying motivation for asking you personal questions.

Finally, do not share personal information with a client who is sociopathic and/or a skilled manipulator. These individuals are adept at detecting other people's weaknesses and will often take advantage of these.

Responding Assertively To Clients

There are several appropriate reasons why you might respond assertively to a client. First, when you are appropriately decisive, a client usually develops more confidence in you and is more willing to accept your assistance. Second, skilled assertive responding can allow you to facilitate certain treatment processes, methods, and situations. For example, assertiveness is necessary for the following (Hepworth et al., 2006):

- Issuing directives. Rather than making tentative requests, such as, "Is it okay with you if we explore your relationship with your mother some more?," you would want to say, "Let's go back to what you said about your mother because I think it's important."

- Confronting or challenging a client when doing so will further therapeutic goals.

- Interrupting dysfunctional interactions in family or couples therapy sessions.

- Maintaining focus in an interview and handling interruptions and distractions.

- Openly addressing a client's anger. You could reflect her anger and any other underlying feelings, explore the situation that made her angry, authentically share your response to the anger (e.g., use an I-statement), and, when necessary, help the client resolve the circumstances that made her angry.

- Setting limits and saying "no" to a client. This may be necessary, for instance, if a client is manipulative, asks to see you socially, is overly dependent upon you, is repeatedly late or absent, fails to pay you, expresses herself in an abusive way, or comes to a session intoxicated.

Finally, as with authenticity, when you respond in an assertive manner, you provide the client with a model for relating assertively with you and with others.

Using I-Statements

As noted previously, **I-statements** can be useful for managing situations of confrontation or conflict with a client and turning them into opportunities for the client to grow. Using an I-statement with a client allows you to express your feelings of disappointment, frustration, anger, etc., in a manner that minimizes the chances that the client will become defensive or argue with you. For example, with a client who has missed several sessions without calling to cancel beforehand, you might use an I-statement that has the following elements:

- first, the feelings you experience as a result of the behavior (e.g., "I feel disappointed when you ...");
- second, the specific behavior that has elicited these feelings (the client's failure to show up for/cancel the sessions); and
- third, the tangible impact of the behavior (e.g., your schedule gets disrupted).

For more information on I-statements, see Section IV in Interventions with Clients/Client Systems.

Using Humor With Clients

When used in a timely way, humor that stems from empathic listening and reflects a positive outlook can be an effective helping skill. Context is the most important consideration for the use of humor with your clients. For example, using humor when a client (without serious psychopathology) expresses a limited view of a situation has the potential for promoting growth and change by offering another perspective. The use of humor when a client is in pain, however, is countertherapeutic and could result in the client experiencing feelings of devaluation and humiliation, which could lead to a range of negative feelings including anger. In addition, it is usually unwise to use humor before rapport is well established.

D. Transference and Countertransference

1. Transference: The concept of transference, which originated in psychoanalytic theory, is used by some social workers, particularly those who are psychodynamically oriented, as a tool for understanding and helping clients work through their past conflicts. Transference refers to emotional reactions that are assigned to current relationships but have their roots in earlier, often unresolved and unconscious experiences. For example, a client who grew up feeling hostility toward her parents may develop hostile feelings toward you, even though no overt reason exists for these feelings (Barker, 2003). Transference may be either positive or negative, however: With **positive transference**, a client transfers affectionate feelings to her social worker; and with **negative transference**, a client transfers hostile feelings to her social worker.

Recent modifications to Freud's psychoanalytic theory include a reconceptualization of transference (and countertransference). With regard to transference, some experts suggest that transference is not a distortion (which is what Freud maintained), but, instead, the client's response to the therapist's actual behavior and an attempt to instill that behavior with personal meaning (Gil, 1982).

To manage a client's transference reaction, you may do the following: (a) First consider the possibility that the client's reaction is realistic. (b) If you conclude that the client expects you to respond in countertherapeutic ways as others in her life have, respond differently in order to disprove her expectations. The client will then have to deal with you as a real person. (c) Help the client identify the source of her distorted perception by exploring how and why her feelings evolved. Don't try to change her distortion immediately. (d) After the client recognizes the distortion underlying her feelings, share your own feelings. (e) After problematic feelings have been explored, help the client figure out whether she has had similar reactions in other relationships.

2. Countertransference: Countertransference is defined as "a set of conscious or unconscious emotional reactions to a client experienced by the social worker ... usually in a clinical setting" (Barker, 2003, p. 100). Like transference, the concept of countertransference originated in psychoanalytic theory. In Freud's initial conceptualization, countertransference was considered to reflect the therapist's distorted response to a client. Recent conceptualizations maintain that, when countertransference is recognized and appropriately managed, it is a potential source of information about the client and an important contributor to the curative process (Langs, 1982).

As a social worker, you should seek the advice and counsel of colleagues whenever consultation is in the best interests of a client. In the case of countertransference, you should seek consultation *before* countertransference feelings and their potential consequences (such as the loss of objectivity) have a chance to damage your relationship with a client or otherwise interfere with treatment.

IV. Supervision in Social Work

A. Overview of Supervision

Kadushin and Harkness (2002, p. 23) define supervision in social work as "the process of overseeing, directing, coordinating, enhancing, and evaluating the on-the-job performance of workers for whom the supervisor is responsible."

Supervision is used to train and support beginning workers and as a means of quality control in the delivery of services. Ultimately, supervision is performed for the benefit of the service rather than for the worker. Its effectiveness is measured by the extent to which efforts to help workers improve their job performance result in better service and improved worker ability to respond to clients' needs.

The short-term objectives of supervision are to (a) provide workers with the work structure and agency resources that enable them to do their jobs effectively (administrative supervision); (b) increase workers' knowledge, skills, and ability to do their jobs effectively and help workers develop professionally so that one day they can function without supervision (educational supervision); and (c) sustain workers emotionally in the performance of their jobs (supportive supervision).

The long-term objective of supervision is to provide clients the most efficient and effective service possible consistent with agency policies and procedures. The short-term objectives contribute to achieving this long-term objective.

The Supervisor's Functions

The three basic functions of supervision – administrative, educational, and supportive – reflect the three short-term objectives of supervision (see above) and their ultimate purpose is to enable workers to provide clients with the best possible service. Each supervisory function introduced below will be discussed more thoroughly later in this section.

1. Administrative Function: The administrative tasks of supervision require managerial skills. The supervisor is responsible for providing workers with the work structure and access to agency resources that allow them to do their jobs well. She is concerned with such issues as the workers' productivity, progress on cases, and workload and whether they are following the agency's procedures.

Most supervisors focus heavily on administrative tasks because these tasks play an important role in fulfilling the accountability demands faced by their agency. Additionally, improving worker productivity and efficiency has become increasingly important as a result of reductions in funding for social service programs and changes in social welfare policy (e.g., fewer available resources, reduced staff).

2. Educational Function: The educational tasks of supervision require teaching and technical skills. The supervisor is charged with providing the training that allows workers to achieve their objectives and the skills that prepare them to do their jobs more effectively and independently.

a. Training Approaches in Education Supervision: In educational supervision, a tutorial (or teaching) model is commonly used with workers who have little professional experience. More experienced workers also receive training through case consultation, peer-group interactions, and service delivery teams (these approaches are described later in this section).

In addition, a supervisor may switch between the role of educator and the role of consultant based on a worker's needs – i.e., with an experienced worker, the supervisor may set aside her educational role and serve more as a consultant on a challenging case.

b. Educational Supervision vs. In-Service Training and Staff Development: Staff development encompasses all of the procedures an agency uses to improve the job-related knowledge, skills, and attitudes of its staff, including educational supervision and in-service training. Examples of staff development activities include training sessions, lectures, workshops, reading material, and discussion groups. **In-service training** is formal training that is planned in advance and provided to a circumscribed group of personnel at an agency who have the same job responsibilities or the same job classification. The content taught at an in-service training applies to all members of the group but is specifically relevant to none of them.

In contrast, educational supervision provides training that is tailored to the needs of a specific worker who has a specific caseload and is dealing with specific problems (i.e., the program of education is individualized to meet the needs of this worker). Through educational supervision, a supervisor helps a worker apply the generic training offered by in-service training.

3. Supportive Function: The supportive tasks of supervision call for interpersonal skills. The supervisor is responsible for making sure workers have the psychological and interpersonal resources needed to operate effectively on an emotional level. This allows workers to do their job more effectively and derive satisfaction from their work.

The Supervisor's Position Within the Agency

1. Connecting the Work Group and Management: The supervisor holds a middle-management position within an agency. She is a member of both the work group and management:

- The supervisor is responsible for the on-the-job performance of direct service workers as well as accountable to the agency's administrative directors.

- The supervisor serves as the link or "bridge" between the agency's direct service workers and administrators: The supervisor (a) helps workers and administrators communicate with each other (e.g., she tells administrators how effectively agency services are being delivered and tells workers about changes administrators have made to the agency's policies); (b) advocates for workers with administrators and vice versa (e.g., she translates workers' concerns to administrators and vice versa); and (c) resolves conflict and distrust between workers and administrators without taking the side of either group (e.g., she tries to understand each group's needs and negotiates between their differing needs – i.e., workers need autonomy, while administrators are concerned with accountability).

2. Executive Administrators' vs. Supervisors' Management Tasks: An agency's executive administrators focus on the stability and survival of the agency as a whole. Their tasks include policy formulation, program planning, agency funding, and community relations; they strive to protect the agency's reputation in the eyes of outsiders.

The managerial tasks of supervisors include program management and program implementation – i.e., supervisors transform policies and objectives into tasks and then assign these tasks to workers. The supervisor is focused on the environment within the agency and the work being done there and interacts daily with front-line staff.

Supervisory Authority

1. Power Types Underlying Supervisory Authority: "Power" refers to the ability to implement one's authority. The types of power underlying a supervisor's (or other leader's) authority include the following (French & Raven, 1959).

Reward power: This form of power stems from the ability to control tangible rewards (raises, work assignments, etc.) and psychic rewards (e.g., praise). For reward power to be effective, workers must believe that their supervisor has authority to make decisions concerning rewards, and it must be apparent to workers that rewards are distributed based on job performance.

Coercive power: This type of power derives from the ability to control tangible punishments (demotion, poor performance rating, etc.) and psychic punishments (criticism, disapproval). For coercive power to be effective, workers must believe that the supervisor is likely to take disciplinary action.

Legitimate/positional power: This form of power stems from the authority associated with the position of supervisor, regardless of the person holding the position – i.e., the workers believe that the supervisor, simply because of her position, has a legitimate right to expect workers to follow her authority.

Referent power: Referent power derives from a worker's identification with the supervisor and eagerness to be like her and liked by her. Having a positive relationship with a worker provides a supervisor with a source of power for influencing the worker's behavior and attitudes. When workers identify with their supervisor, they internalize her expectations.

Expert power: Expert power exists when the supervisor has special knowledge and skills that her supervisees need. This form of power is confined to areas in which the supervisor has expertise and it can diminish as a worker's own expertise grows and he relies less on the supervisor for help. Expert power may also stem from the supervisor's expert knowledge of the policies, procedures, and operations in the agency.

2. Compliance vs. Internalization and Conformity: Compliance occurs when a person changes his behavior in order to obtain a reward or avoid punishment; compliance is public and does not involve a private change in opinions or attitudes. Reward power and coercive power usually produce compliance and a change in behavior, particularly when a worker knows he is being observed.

In contrast, internalization occurs when a person changes his behavior because he actually (privately) accepts the beliefs, attitudes, or behaviors of another person. Expert power and referent power are more effective for producing conformity – i.e., both attitudinal conformity (which implies an internalization of influence) and overt behavioral conformity.

3. Formal Power and Functional Power: The five sources of power defined above have been classified into two groups – formal and functional:

- Formal power is related to the title/position a supervisor (or other leader) holds and the authority delegated to that position. Formal power is acquired automatically when a person becomes a supervisor, and there is little difference between supervisors in the same agency in regard to their formal power. Formal power includes legitimate/positional, reward, and coercive power.

- Functional power depends on the person holding the position of supervisor. Functional power has to be earned (and continuously re-earned) by the supervisor, and there may be big differences between supervisors at the same agency in regard to their functional power because of differences in their expertise and interpersonal skills. Functional power includes expert and referent power.

Problems tend to arise when a person with formal power, such as a supervisor, lacks sufficient functional power (e.g., when she knows less than or has not gained the respect of those under her authority).

4. Guidelines for Using Supervisory Authority: Important guidelines for using supervisory authority effectively include the following (Kadushin & Harkness, 2002):

- The supervisor should exercise authority only when doing so is necessary to achieve objectives she and the worker have agreed upon.

- The supervisor should exercise authority in a predictable manner.

- The supervisor should exercise authority impartially.

- The supervisor should communicate to workers the reasons underlying a directive and be available to discuss it with them.

- The supervisor should use the least amount of authority needed to accomplish the objectives of supervision (e.g., simply providing information may be sufficient for inducing a worker to change his behavior in the desired direction).

5. Informed Consents From Clients: When a client gives informed consent to receive supervised services, she grants oversight authority to the worker's supervisor. In this context, "informing" the client means providing her with information about the supervisor's qualifications; the supervisor's and the worker's goals, methods, and responsibilities; and the relevant limits to confidentiality.

6. What Workers Expect From Their Supervisor: Generally, workers expect their supervisor to do the following things (e.g., Kadushin & Harkness, 2002; Sheafor & Horejsi, 2003):

- Keep them informed about agency policy, including changes in policy.

- Monitor their work to make sure it is in compliance with agency policy.
- Coordinate the work of agency staff so that they can achieve their objectives.
- Help them develop new skills.
- Be available for consultation on difficult cases.
- Evaluate their job performance.
- Redirect their efforts when they make a mistake or need help to perform their work more effectively.
- Give them support when they need it.
- Facilitate cooperation among staff.
- Mediate their disagreements and conflicts with one another.
- Communicate their needs to the agency's administrators.

B. Individual Supervision and Group Supervision

Individual Supervision

The individual supervisory conference is the most common kind of meeting between supervisors and workers, but, in many agencies, individual supervision is supplemented by other forms of supervision, especially group supervision. When that arrangement is used with a group of workers, the same supervisor is generally responsible for both individual and group conferences. One reason for this is that individual and group supervision should complement each other – that is, the content of group conferences may be based on problems that are discussed repeatedly in workers' individual conferences, and discussions from group supervisory meetings may be referred to in subsequent individual supervisory meetings in which a worker's own case situations are addressed.

1. The Supervisor's Activities: In the course of providing individual supervision to a worker, a supervisor may (a) review the worker's entire caseload over the course of multiple conferences so that all cases receive some attention; (b) review the worker's cases selectively (e.g., check 25 percent of the worker's caseload); (c) review only cases with which the worker is having (or is likely to have) difficulty; or (d) review only cases the worker selects for review. Individual conferences are usually scheduled in advance and occur on a regular basis, but impromptu conferences can be held when a worker faces a crisis with a client.

2. Preparing for an Individual Conference: Each individual conference must have a clearly defined purpose which has been determined in advance. Before a conference, the worker gives the supervisor some record of his current work (e.g., written records, case files, reports, work plan). The supervisor reviews this material, verifying that the worker is complying with agency procedure in delivering service (an administrative supervisory task) and checking for performance weaknesses that require training (an educational supervisory task). Based on this review, the supervisor develops a teaching plan for the upcoming conference or series of conferences. Ideally, the selected training objectives relate to the worker's job activities and the chosen teaching approach is consistent with the worker's learning needs and patterns.

3. Holding an Individual Conference: For educational purposes, the individual conference is essentially a tutorial in which the supervisor provides education and feedback to the worker. (See the review of Educational Supervision in this section for more information on teaching and feedback.) A conference focusing on a worker's clinical work will usually emphasize management of the case (e.g., increasing understanding of the client and the client's situation, planning intervention strategies, etc.) and further development of the worker's knowledge, skills, and professional identity. Under no circumstances shoul the supervisor provide therapy to the worker. However, it is appropriate for the supervisor to point out where personal issues may be interfering with the social worker's work, and if not resolved may suggest seeking personal therapy to resolve the issue.

Group Supervision

The group supervisory conference is a meeting between a supervisor and a group of workers who fall under the supervisor's administrative authority; a typical group includes four or five workers. In some agencies, the group conference is the main form of supervision; in most agencies, group supervision is used along with individual supervision.

1. Purpose and Content of Group Conferences: As with individual conferences, group conferences are scheduled ahead of time to take place on a regular basis and their content is planned in advance. Each group conference should have a clearly defined purpose.

Clinical case material is typically used to stimulate group discussions. The supervisor may help a worker select (and, sometimes, prepare) a case for presentation; this case should be one that has the potential to provide valuable training to all the workers in the group. Planning for the **case presentation** occurs in the worker's individual supervisory conferences. Ideally, the case presentation will focus on general content that all workers in the group can apply to case situations in their caseload rather than on specific planning for the case under discussion (specific planning is more appropriate to the worker's individual supervisory conferences).

Examples of content that may be covered in group supervision meetings include interviewing clients, recording procedures, referral procedures, caseload management, worker-client interactions, ethics, communications from administration (e.g., about changes to agency policy), and problems that workers want administration to know about.

2. Leading the Group: The supervisor has primary responsibility for leading the supervisory group, but the group as a whole shares responsibility for decisions about the group's purpose and function. Ideally, the supervisor will exercise the least amount of leadership necessary to assure that the group achieves its objectives. Over the life of the group, the supervisor should become progressively less active and allow the workers to take over more leadership activities.

3. Advantages of Group Supervision: According to Kadushin and Harkness (2002, pp. 391-399), the advantages of group supervision include the following:

- More efficient and cost-effective use of administrative time and effort.
- Efficient use of a greater variety of teaching approaches (e.g., films).

- Workers have an opportunity to share their experiences with similar job-related problems and solutions.

- Workers can receive emotional support from members of the group.

- Morale increases when workers share common job-related problems (i.e., the group provides universalization and normalization).

- Workers can measure their relative competence by viewing others' work.

- Some (but not all) workers are more comfortable learning in a group setting.

- Some workers need "safety in numbers" to challenge their supervisor (e.g., to voice objections to what she is saying).

- Encouragement of interaction and peer-group cohesion among workers in a unit.

- The supervisor can observe how workers interact in a group.

- The group format can make it easier for a supervisor to fulfill her role responsibilities when they conflict. For example, while the supervisor is informing a worker about task expectations (instrumental role), the group can communicate support (expressive role). (See also the review of Supportive Supervision in this section.)

- It can be easier to modify a worker's behavior when members of his peer group have supported the supervisor's point of view. (This does not apply to noncompliant behavior requiring a reprimand, however – such behavior should be dealt with in private.)

- Workers can observe the supervisor in a group and learn group-interaction skills from her.

- A racially mixed group provides opportunities for multicultural learning.

- Group supervision offers a transitional step toward independence from supervision (e.g., initially, a worker may receive primarily individual supervision and only a limited amount of group supervision; as he progresses, he may receive less and less individual supervision and more and more group supervision in its place).

4. Disadvantages of Group Supervision: According to Kadushin and Harkness (2002, pp. 399-402), the disadvantages of group supervision include the following:

- The primary disadvantage is that group conferences must focus on the general, shared needs of all workers in the group. A group conference can't address the specific needs of any one worker (e.g., it can't examine how one worker can apply the learning to his own caseload).

- There may be obstacles to learning if interpersonal conflict develops between/among workers in the group.

- It can be difficult to incorporate a newly hired worker into an existing supervisory group.

- Whereas an individual conference presses a worker to arrive at his own solutions and decisions, the group format allows him to avoid this responsibility and rely on the group's solutions and decisions.

- If a worker is anxious about hearing critical feedback, the multiple sources of feedback available in the group can be a problem.

- The supervisor has to communicate in a way that is meaningful to all group members. Framing a message in a way that allows multiple workers to understand it can prevent the supervisor from meeting all the particular needs of any one individual worker.

- Because there are several workers and one supervisor, the workers may organize against the supervisor or the supervisor may otherwise lose of control of a meeting.

- If the group is highly cohesive, the members may feel pressured to conform to group thinking (i.e., **groupthink** may begin to operate). While such uniform thinking may influence individual workers to accept agency procedures, etc., it also tends to suppress innovation and individuality. To lessen groupthink, a supervisor should, among other things, encourage and support the expression of diverse ideas within the group.

C. Supervision Procedures

Procedures for Observing Workers' Performance

A worker's written records and verbal reports are the most common sources of information about the worker's performance and both are second-hand and subject to distortions. Supervision procedures involving observation of a worker interacting with clients give the supervisor a more direct way of learning about the worker's performance. Ethically, a social worker must have the client's permission for any procedure that allows a supervisor (or other third party) to observe the client-worker interaction, as well as before audiotaping or videotaping an interview with the client or letting a supervisor (or other third party) view the recordings.

1. Direct Observation Procedures: Direct observation procedures used by supervisors include the following:

Sitting in: The supervisor sits in on an interview (or group session) as just an observer.

One-way mirrors: The supervisor watches the interview from behind a one-way mirror. She can see and hear the interaction but cannot be seen or heard by the worker or client.

Co-therapy supervision: The supervisor sits in on an interview, but the worker is in charge of the interaction with the client. The supervisor intervenes only when the worker has difficulty, the worker indicates that he wants help, or the supervisor sees an opportunity to model behavior that the worker needs to learn.

2. Observation via Audio/Video Recordings: Audio and video recordings of worker-client interactions provide reliable information about the worker's performance that can be studied and discussed during his supervisory conferences.

3. Live Supervision During Interviews: With most other observation procedures, a worker's performance is discussed after the client interview has taken place (this is called "post-hoc" supervision). In contrast, with live supervision, the supervisor observes an interview in real time and is able to give the worker immediate feedback. The supervisor's interventions may be either general statements or specific directions for action; and either highly directive (telling the worker to do something) or delivered in the form of suggestion ("It might help if you ..."). Generally, a supervisor's interventions are more concrete and more directive with beginning workers and more general and less directive with experienced workers. Other supervisor interventions in live supervision may be supportive statements that praise something the worker is doing in the interview.

A supervisor providing live supervision may either sit in on the interview or watch it through a one-way mirror or video camera pickup. Traditional live supervision formats have included "knock-on-the-door" supervision and "bug-in-the-ear" supervision (in which the worker wears an earphone in one ear, through which he receives immediate feedback). More current formats, including "**bug-in-the-eye**" (**BITE**) **supervision**, rely more on computer technology (Jakob, Weck, & Bohus, 2013). With BITE supervision, the supervisor follows an interview online with the help of a video camera, and her suggestions and interventions appear on a computer monitor that only the worker can see. The worker can decide for himself when to look at the monitor and whether to use the suggestions.

One important advantage of live supervision is that it protects client welfare. Significant drawbacks are that it can be disruptive (although BITE supervision is much less so) and that it has the potential to produce workers who take too little initiative (Kadushin & Harkness, 2002).

Procedures for Increasing Worker Autonomy

1. Peer Group Supervision: Peer group supervision may supplement traditional supervision but should not replace it. In peer group supervision, "A group of professionals in the same agency meet regularly to review cases and treatment approaches without a leader, share expertise and take responsibility for their own and each other's professional development and for maintaining standards of [agency] service" (Hare & Frankena, 1972, p. 527). Peer group supervision tends to be most useful when the group is made up of workers of comparable experience, length of training, and background (Schreiber & Frank, 1983).

Compared to traditional group supervision, peer group supervision offers workers a greater degree of independence. The workers control peer group supervision meetings, and, if a supervisor attends the meetings, she is just another member of the group. Workers decide for themselves what to do with the suggestions and advice offered by their peers.

2. Peer Consultation: Peer consultation is most effective when the involved peers have about equal levels of competence. In this way, the workers have equal status, and the consultee on one case can serve as the consultant on another case.

3. Participatory Management: Having workers participate more in management can improve morale and prevent burnout. The following are examples of participatory management approaches.

a. Team Service Delivery: In this approach, a team of workers is given responsibility for performing the main tasks of supervision. The group, as a whole, is responsible for work assignments, monitoring team members' work, and meeting the educational needs of team members. The supervisor is just one more member of the team, though she does have slightly higher status than the workers – she serves as a consultant, coordinator, resource person, and, when necessary, as a team leader. And, while the group is authorized to make decisions, final decisions have to be approved by the supervisor who has ultimate administrative responsibility for the team's decisions and actions.

b. Management by Objectives: In management by objectives (MBO) (or, in this case, "**supervision by objectives**"), the supervisor and worker jointly establish precise, measurable objectives for each case: (a) During conferences, the supervisor and worker define the objectives, set a time limit for achieving the objectives, and arrange the objectives in order of priority; (b) the supervisor, with active participation by the worker, then monitors work toward the objectives; and (c) when the time limit has expired, the supervisor and worker evaluate the worker's performance by determining the extent to which he achieved the objectives in each case.

c. Quality Circles: Quality circles are voluntary groups of workers created to identify, study, and solve work-related problems. In social work, for example, staff members who work in related areas may meet monthly to address problems associated with their work (productivity, service, etc.). Underlying the use of quality circles is an effort to promote a more humanistic, democratic, and collaborative relationship between workers and management.

D. Administrative Supervision

The administrative function of supervision focuses on providing workers with the agency resources and the structure they need to do their jobs well.

Tasks of Administrative Supervision

The tasks of administrative supervision are described below (Kadushin & Harkness, 2002).

1. Recruit, Hire, Induct, and Place Workers: Because they interact daily with workers, supervisors can provide valuable help in defining the key job tasks of different positions, developing criteria for hiring, and applying these criteria during applicant interviews. Supervisors don't usually make final hiring decisions, but they do make hiring recommendations which are taken into consideration in the selection process.

The task of inducting and placing a new or newly hired worker includes, among other things, meeting with the worker to discuss matters such as the function of the unit in which he will work, the nature of supervision, and the first tasks he might be assigned, informing others in the unit that the worker has been hired, finding him a desk, and introducing him to others employed at the agency.

Sometimes work groups respond poorly to personnel changes and have difficulty accepting new members. Supervisors will generally take a "wait-and-see" attitude before calling a meeting to discuss this problem in a formal way. After some time has passed, the supervisor can then decide whether she needs to take specific action to correct the problem.

2. Develop a Unit Work Plan: Planning the work includes (a) dividing the workload and allocating available resources so that the unit can complete its work effectively and in a timely way (e.g., no worker is overloaded, no overtime is necessary); and (b) preparing a unit budget based on an estimation of the unit's upcoming workload and the fiscal, technical, and human resources that will be needed to complete it. (A "unit budget" is a component of the total agency budget.) To plan work effectively, a supervisor must be familiar with her supervisees, the cases requiring action, and the tasks the unit is excepted to achieve. She must also act as a gatekeeper, making sure that all cases assigned by administration to her unit are appropriate given the unit's functions and expertise.

3. Assign and Delegate the Work:

a. Assign the Work: Assigning the work involves selecting tasks for individual workers based on the unit work plan. When assigning tasks to workers, the supervisor in a social agency usually considers the following variables:

- The supervisor takes into account each worker's strengths and weaknesses.

- The supervisor considers each worker's current caseload in terms of the number of cases, their difficulty, and the challenge of each new assignment. The goal is to equalize, as much as possible, the demands made on workers who have the same title and salary level.

- Although some workers prefer to work repeatedly on similar tasks, most workers get more satisfaction from working on a variety of job assignments. Thus, whenever possible, supervisors afford workers variety in their job assignments, including in job tasks, cases, and problem situations.

- Workers are more motivated and learn more when they are challenged by their work. Thus, the supervisor tries to avoid assigning tasks that are clearly below the level of a worker's capacity.

- When possible, the supervisor allows workers to express their preference for particular kinds of case situations, and, when necessary, the supervisor considers whether to match worker and client regarding age, gender, race, or ethnicity.

- If a worker says he would prefer not to work on a particular case, a supervisor will usually help the worker examine his feelings about the case. Sometimes, it will turn out that the case should not be assigned to the worker because of his strong negative feelings.

b. Delegate the Work: Delegating the work involves informing workers about how the work will be done. With an experienced worker, a supervisor often will just define the objectives and allow the worker to determine for himself what actions to take to achieve the objectives. With a less experienced worker, a supervisor usually retains more responsibility for how the work is done – she may require the worker to get her approval before taking any action or she may simply tell the worker in advance what actions to take. Additionally, supervisors may give workers less decision-making discretion when the client is a member of a highly vulnerable population, when an error in judgment could have serious consequences for the client, or when a decision would result in the commitment of limited agency resources.

An important concept associated with delegating work to supervisees is something known as the "**respondeat superior doctrine**" (**vicarious liability**), which defines the legal liability of supervisors for the job-related actions of their supervisees: A supervisor may be held liable, along with the supervisee, for any actions on the part of the supervisee that harm a client. That is, a supervisor, by definition, retains administrative authority over the people under her supervision, and, as a consequence, she is ultimately responsible for the actions of her supervisees. In other words, by delegating a task, a supervisor shares some of her authority with a supervisee, who may be empowered to make decisions and take action when doing the assigned task; the supervisor, however, retains *ultimate* responsibility for the work she assigns and delegates and for the decisions and actions of her supervisees (this does not mean, however, that supervisees bear no responsibility for their actions). When a supervisee takes an action, it is presumed that the supervisor has reviewed and approved it; if the action is performed incompetently, the supervisor is responsible for having delegated the action to a worker who she should have known was not competent to perform it.

4. Coordinate the Work: The supervisor tries to maximize cooperation and coordinated effort and minimize conflict among workers and work units at her agency and with other social service agencies in the community. For instance, she (a) makes sure that workers have access to the human, fiscal, and physical resources they need to do their jobs (e.g., makes psychiatric consultation available to workers); (b) makes sure that workers understand and accept the goals and objectives of the agency; and (c) resolves conflicts between workers in her unit and between her unit and other units.

5. Monitor, Review, and Evaluate Worker Performance: This task includes the following components:

- The supervisor verifies that workers are available to cover the workload. She is concerned, in particular, with assuring continuity of service if a worker leaves the agency and continuity of contact and work coverage when a worker is absent.

- The supervisor reviews task assignments to verify that they are being accomplished, completed on time and in a manner consistent with agency policies and procedures, and accomplished at a minimally acceptable level. To monitor and review work, the supervisor gets verbal reports from workers, reads records, and reviews statistical reports.

- The supervisor is responsible for formal performance appraisals of workers. (These evaluations are described later in this section.)

- If a worker's performance is clearly unsatisfactory, the supervisor takes disciplinary action.

6. Communicate Information and Feedback: Adequate and effective communication within the agency is a key determinant of worker satisfaction. In a traditional social work setting, communication occurs in the following ways:

- The supervisor communicates to workers what administrators want workers to know about the agency's objectives, policies, procedures, and structure, including proposed and upcoming changes. The supervisor must make sure that these messages are understood and accepted by workers and should motivate workers to behave in a manner consistent with the information. This reflects a **downward channel** of communication.

- Workers depend on their supervisor to communicate their needs "up" through the agency to administrators who can make changes and meet workers' needs. This reflects an **upward channel** of communication.

- Similarly, administrators depend on the supervisor for information about how agency policies and procedures are being implemented, problems in implementation, successes, and workers' feelings about agency objectives, policies, and procedures.

- The supervisor communicates laterally (horizontally) within the agency and with other agencies and between her unit and other units through her peers at the supervisory level. Communication between supervisors is important for addressing such issues as conflict and overlap, coordination of work, duplication of services, attaining resources, making referrals, and integrating services. Lateral channels of communication are based on a need to cooperate so that work can be coordinated and, unlike vertical channels, they are not hierarchical.

- Not all communications are through formal channels. Instead, communication networks also operate through an agency's informal structure. Informal communication among peers is an important source of education and support. A supervisor should address gossip or rumors circulating among staff only if the rumors are likely to damage morale and/or she needs to correct inaccurate or false information.

Of course, not all information from administrators should be communicated automatically to workers, and not everything shared by workers needs to be communicated to administration. Instead, the supervisor should be selective (e.g., she should communicate information that helps workers do their jobs more effectively).

Finally, a supervisor has available a range of ways to communicate information (upward or downward), including face-to-face communication, phone calls, and writing e-mails, memos, or reports. A supervisor may use several channels to communicate the same information, in part, because repeated transmission of the same information is effective for increasing people's understanding of the message and minimizing the chances of miscommunication or message distortion.

7. Advocate for Staff: The supervisor advocates for staff with administration, other units, and other agencies. She should actively represent workers' interests to administrators and advocate for necessary changes. Administrators tend to be more responsive to a supervisor's efforts in this regard when the supervisor outlines the problem clearly and suggests alternative solutions for consideration.

8. Be an Administrative "Buffer": This task includes the following components:

- Administration expects supervisors to handle service-related problems (e.g., to deal with clients who have complaints about someone other than a worker or who are unhappy with a worker's decision and want to speak to someone with greater authority).

- The supervisor acts as a buffer between workers and the agency (e.g., she protects workers from unrealistic workloads imposed by administration and she helps workers understand and negotiate the agency's organizational hierarchy).

- The supervisor protects workers from sexual harassment within her work unit.

- The supervisor protects the agency from potentially damaging behavior by workers or other employees (e.g., from activities that could undermine the agency's standing with its donor constituency and, thereby, threaten its survival).

- The supervisor protects and preserves the agency's belief system.

With regard to the latter, the NASW Code of Ethics says that social workers should not allow an employing organization's policies, procedures, regulations, or administrative orders to interfere with their ethical practice of social work. If a conflict arises, a supervisor should meet with the worker to discuss the worker's questions and concerns and help him understand the rationale underlying the agency's mission or operations. Even if a supervisor disagrees with an agency policy, rule, or procedure, she should generally encourage workers to comply with it.

9. Be an Agent for Change and a Community Liaison: The supervisor may participate in developing or changing agency policy using information gleaned from her ongoing contact with workers. As a "middle manager," the supervisor is in a good position to influence administration to make changes as well as influence workers to accept changes. Workers are more likely to accept change if (a) they participate from the beginning in planning the change, (b) they are told early about the nature of the planned change, (c) the change is introduced slowly (ideally with an initial trial effort), (d) expectations are made clear, (e) the change is consistent with agency norms and objectives, (f) there is some guarantee that the change will have the predicted effect, (g) supervisors and other administrators communicate a strong belief in the desirability of the change, (h) supervisors and other administrators acknowledge and demonstrate empathy for the difficulties that the change produces for the staff, and (i) action is taken to minimize the costs of the change to the staff (Kadushin & Harkness, 2002).

Additionally, if the supervisor is aware of a lack in the community social service system of a service that would increase the effectiveness of her supervisees' work, she should advocate in the community for support for the service.

Noncompliance and Disciplinary Action

Most supervisors realize that a certain amount of noncompliance with agency rules, standards, and procedures will occur; they also know that certain procedures can be ignored sometimes without harming the agency or client. In fact, by helping staff understand the purpose of agency rules and procedures, supervisors can prevent workers from applying them in rigid, mechanical ways, rather than in ways that best serve their clients.

1. Noncompliance Due to a Lack of Information or Skill: If a worker is noncompliant because he doesn't know or understand what is expected of him, a supervisor will usually clarify for the worker what is required by agency policy. If a worker understands what is expected of him, but can't meet these demands because he lacks sufficient knowledge or skill, then education and training are called for. In these situations, clarification, education, and training, rather than criticism or sanctions, should be used to obtain compliance.

2. Taking Disciplinary Action in Response to Noncompliance: Supervisors sometimes need to apply sanctions to compel workers to comply with agency policy, rules, and procedures. Examples of situations in which sanctions may be needed include when a worker repeatedly misses deadlines, is frequently absent or late, fails to turn in reports, disrupts others' work by gossiping too much, is careless with agency resources, or is rude to clients.

Guidelines for taking disciplinary action in response to noncompliance include the following:

- In all cases, a supervisor's objective in applying a sanction should be preventative and corrective, rather than punitive.

- A supervisor should respond in a timely way the first time a worker chooses to be noncompliant with an agency policy, rule, or procedure (e.g., when a worker knows what's expected of him but chooses not to do it). It's more difficult for a supervisor to take effective corrective action if she has initially ignored a worker's noncompliant behavior.

- A supervisor should discuss in private any behavior that calls for a reprimand. To criticize a worker in front of his peers makes it more difficult to help him change the behavior; it also makes it more difficult for the worker to respond appropriately to the criticism.

- When delivering a reprimand, a supervisor should be impersonal, consistent, specific, and factual.

- The reprimand is best delivered at a time when the supervisor is not upset. (A delay is recommended for calming down and ensuring privacy, but the delay should be as short as possible because it is best to deal with noncompliant behavior in a timely way.)

- A reprimand tends to be more effective when the supervisor also communicates concern for the worker, listens to the worker's explanation of the situation and tries to understand how he sees it, and conveys a desire to help the worker improve or change. In other words, a reprimand should be directed toward behavioral change that will improve the worker's, as well as the agency's, effectiveness.

- Behaviors requiring a reprimand as well as the corrective action should be recorded so that, if the behavior recurs, there is a record to justify further action.

- Following are the corrective or disciplinary actions a supervisor may take, listed from least to most severe: a review of the situation with the worker; a warning; a verbal reprimand if the behavior continues; a written reprimand placed in the worker's file; a lower-than-average evaluation rating; suspension for a limited period; demotion; and dismissal (Kadushin & Harkness, 2002).

- The supervisor should document all serious disciplinary actions (e.g., suspension without pay, demotion, firing) because she will need to defend the action in the event of a grievance procedure.

- Termination (dismissal) is uncommon, but it may be justified when a worker's performance is clearly inadequate, clearly unethical, or clearly and consistently in violation of agency policies or procedures. In most agencies, the worker's supervisor would be the one responsible for firing the worker.

Finally, when noncompliance by a worker is not adequately resolved at the supervisory level, it may become necessary to take the problem to the policy decision-making level of the agency. When this happens, all workers in the agency are affected (e.g., their autonomy may be reduced) because of the actions of just one person. For this reason, workers usually support their supervisors in their efforts to sanction individual staff members.

E. Educational Supervision

Educational supervision (also called "clinical supervision") focuses on teaching workers the information, skills, and attitudes they need to have to perform their jobs effectively and safely. **Clinical supervision** is defined as an arrangement in which a more experienced professional supervises the work of a less experienced professional in order to help that professional acquire greater competence in professional performance.

1. Characteristics of Effective Educational Supervision: A productive individual conference in educational supervision generally has the following characteristics:

- The conference is planned and prepared for in advance by both the supervisor and worker.
- The conference has a clear objective, which has been mutually selected by the supervisor and worker.
- The conference focuses on the worker's clinical work.
- The supervisor creates an atmosphere that is optimally suited to learning.
- The supervisor applies effective teaching and learning principles.
- The discussion emphasizes critical analysis by the worker of his own performance with the client, with guidance and input by the supervisor (one of the supervisor's jobs here is to be a resource person for the worker).
- The supervisor provides the worker with clear, relevant feedback that will help him improve his performance.
- There is follow-through, continuity, and connection from one conference to the next.

2. Content in Educational Supervision: Some of the content that workers need to learn is specific to their agency, but other content covers matters that are common to all social work. In particular, supervisors in all agencies generally teach workers about the 4 P's identified by Helen Harris Perlman (1947) – person (client), problem (in social functioning), place (social agency), and process (helping process). Kadushin and Harkness (2002) add a fifth P, suggesting that supervisors should also teach workers about "personnel" (the social worker himself). For each area there are objectives relating to workers' knowledge, skills, and attitudes:

Person: For example, human development and human behavior in response to having the social problems experienced by the agency's clients.

Problem: For example, the causes of social problems, the psychosocial nature of the problems, how the agency's services relate to different problems, local community response to problems, and the effects of a problem on a client system (individual, family, group, community).

Place: For example, the agency's mission and objectives, what kinds of services the agency offers and their eligibility requirements, how agency policy is formulated, how the agency is organized and administered, how the agency fits into the network of social services in the local community, and the agency's statutory authority.

Process: For example, how to help clients deal effectively with social problems, theory that explains why a certain helping technology is likely to work, and the sequential nature and the stages of the helping process.

Personnel: For example, attitudes, feelings, and behaviors that create and sustain effective worker-client relationships; self-awareness; the directed and purposeful use of self; and sensitivity to and awareness of diversity issues including personal biases and prejudices.

3. Teaching Orientations and Procedures: The supervisor's selected teaching approach for a given worker should be based on the fit between the content she needs to teach and the worker's learning preferences. In addition, the supervisor should attempt to generalize the learning beyond the case being discussed.

a. Teaching Orientations: Research (Kadushin, 1990) shows that the best approach to teaching in educational supervision (for both supervisors and workers) involves a fairly balanced mixture of the following two orientations:

Experiential-existential supervisee-centered orientation: The experiential-existential supervisee-centered orientation assumes that a key concern of supervision is the worker's emotional growth and increased self-understanding and self-awareness. When using this approach, the supervisor helps a worker find his own orientation through an ongoing examination of the worker's professional experiences, and the worker plays a major role in determining what he wants to learn. The supervisor forms a relationship with the worker, and their interaction is then akin to the worker-client relationship. The focus is on the worker's feelings about the case, how he does the work, and his relationship to the client. The supervisor reflects, clarifies, probes, and interprets the worker's feelings. Much less emphasis is given to suggestions, advice, and evaluative statements that might influence the worker's behaviors with clients.

Didactic task-centered orientation: The didactic task-centered orientation assumes that a key concern of supervision is the development of the worker's professional skills. The supervisor has primary responsibility for deciding what will be taught, and the focus is on the worker's thinking (rather than on his feelings). Discussions emphasize the content of what the worker is doing with and on behalf of his clients.

b. Teaching Procedures: Supervisors generally use a combination of didactic teaching (e.g., "telling" a worker about the agency's eligibility requirements for services) and dialectical-hypothetical teaching (using questions and comments to help a worker discover his own answers). Other content may be taught through modeling by the supervisor.

c. Social Workers' Learning Orientations: Kolb (1981) found that the learning orientation of most social workers is concrete-active – i.e., social workers seem to prefer learning through active involvement and problem solving by intuitive, trial-and-error means.

4. Feedback From Supervisors: Feedback from supervisors helps workers learn and allows them to correct their performance deficiencies. Guidelines for providing feedback to workers include the following (Kadushin & Harkness, 2002):

- The supervisor should give the feedback as soon as possible after the relevant behavior occurs as this usually increases a worker's motivation to learn.

- The supervisor should be specific – she should name a specific intervention, behavior, or statement by the worker that needs correction or praise.

- The supervisor should be descriptive, not judgmental.

- The supervisor should focus on the behavior of the worker, not on the worker as a person.

- The supervisor should share ideas with the worker, rather than give him advice, and should help the worker explore alternatives, rather than give him answers. She should offer feedback as a suggestion (as something to consider and discuss). She should not require workers to always agree with her feedback.

- The supervisor should make a clear connection between the feedback and what the worker needs to learn. Good feedback targets behavior that can be changed and includes specific suggestions for change.

- The supervisor should be selective – she should be aware of how much feedback a worker can absorb at one time.

5. Parallel Process in Educational Supervision: The "parallel process" (a.k.a. "reflection process") predicts that, in supervisory conferences, a worker will unconsciously re-enact behavior that his client exhibited in an interview. For example, if a client elicited confusion on the part of the worker during an interview, the worker may elicit confusion in his supervisor when he discusses the client's case; or if a client was evasive during an interview, the worker may be evasive during his supervisory conference. The assumption is that the worker unconsciously identifies with and imitates a particular client behavior in an effort to understand it better and get help in dealing with it. Some theorists contend that demonstrations of the parallel process allow the supervisor to perceive more clearly what is going on between a worker and client, and that, in responding therapeutically to the worker "playing the role" of the client, the supervisor can model behavior that the worker can then display therapeutically with his client. (The parallel process can also work in unproductive ways, however – for instance, if a supervisor appears indifferent to a worker, the worker may then reflect this by acting indifferent to his client.) While the parallel process is often discussed in the literature, there is little empirical evidence that it actually exists (Kadushin & Harkness, 2002).

F. Supportive Supervision

Supportive supervision attempts to improve a worker's performance by reducing job-related stress and increasing motivation, job satisfaction, and job commitment.

1. Procedures of Supportive Supervision: In providing supportive supervision, the supervisor generally does the following:

- The supervisor provides the worker with opportunities to succeed on the job and chances to function more independently as his competence continues to grow. Two significant sources of job satisfaction are feelings of achievement and responsibility (Herzberg, 1966).

- The supervisor increases the worker's capacity to handle job stresses. To do so, she uses procedures such as active listening, reassurance, encouragement, approval, praise for achievements, realistic expressions of confidence, catharsis-ventilation, and universalization. Giving unwarranted praise, however, is counterproductive.

- The supervisor helps workers develop a clear understanding of the agency's policies and their goals and role within the agency in order to prevent confusion and uncertainty.

- The supervisor encourages supportive peer-group interaction and cooperative relationships among staff (e.g., she may help organize peer group supervision and peer consultation).

- When necessary, the supervisor advocates with administration for salary increases for staff. Adequate salary levels and benefits are important for increasing job satisfaction and reducing stress.

Note, too, that a supervisor may provide supportive supervision while she's performing administrative or educational functions of her job if she performs those functions in a manner that communicates support to the worker. Moreover, any time a worker receives needed structure or information, this helps reduce his job-related stress by increasing his sense of professional competence.

2. Motivation, Job Commitment, and Leadership Behavior: Sometimes a worker with the structure, knowledge, and skill to do his job well will still perform inadequately because he is not sufficiently motivated or committed to his job. Motivation energizes a worker and keeps him actively involved in his work. "Job commitment" means that a worker is loyal to his agency, believes in the agency's mission, identifies positively with his work group, etc. (Glisson & Durick, 1988).

Research at Ohio State University in the 1940s and 1950s identified two basic and independent dimensions of leadership behavior that can have an impact on workers' motivation and job commitment:

- The first dimension, consideration, refers to the amount of warmth, concern, rapport, and support displayed by the leader. Leaders high in consideration are person-oriented and concerned with the **expressive** aspects of the job.

- Initiating structure, the second dimension, refers to the extent to which a leader defines, directs, and structures her own role and the roles of subordinates. Leaders high in initiating structure are task-oriented and concerned with the **instrumental** aspects of the job.

Although the relationships between consideration, initiating structure, job performance, and job commitment are complex, it appears from the Ohio State studies that the most effective leaders generally are those who score high on *both* dimensions. Thus, supervisors who communicate both support (expressive) and high performance expectations (instrumental) are likely to have the most effective work groups.

3. Worker Burnout: Barker (2003, p. 54) defines burnout as, "... a term used to describe workers who feel apathy or anger as a result of on-the-job stress and frustration. Burnout is found among ... workers who have more responsibility than control." Supervisors need to address burnout in a timely manner because one worker's low morale can spread quickly to others. Moreover, burnout reinforces itself – the symptoms of burnout reduce the chances of succeeding at work, which increases feelings of helplessness, which exacerbates burnout.

a. Symptoms of Burnout: Burnout may include physical, emotional, and/or behavioral symptoms:

- Physical symptoms – e.g., weariness, chronic fatigue, headaches, digestive problems, sleep disturbance, feeling physically drained, being more susceptible to colds.

- Emotional symptoms – e.g., work-related anger, resentment, sense of futility, and/or pessimism; loss of enthusiasm for work; feeling emotionally drained; loss of one's sense of mission and interest in the job.

- Behavioral symptoms – e.g., resistance to going to work; increased tardiness and absenteeism; clock-watching; postponing or canceling appointments with clients; a skeptical or detached manner with clients (distancing oneself emotionally); greater tendency to treat clients in a rigid, mechanical way; having less patience with clients.

b. Causes of Burnout: For social workers, some typical sources of burnout include heavy caseloads; a lack of variety on the job; a lack of therapeutic success; working with many clients in crisis; working with many clients who express strong emotions; working with many involuntary clients who are hostile and resistant; choosing between the competing needs of different clients; physical dangers; pressure to comply with agency policies and procedures (burnout is more common in agencies with a very formalized bureaucratic structure); having their work evaluated by others; threats to their independence; having their decisions reviewed by others (e.g., supervisors, managed care organizations); having responsibilities that exceed their resources and power; ambiguous objectives; high demands for accountability that require them to show clearly how their services make a positive difference in the lives of their clients; frequent re-organization or policy changes at their agency; and a lack of pay equity (i.e., a worker perceives that his pay is inconsistent with his workload, performance, and/or reference group peers).

In addition, more highly concerned, invested, and hard-working workers tend to be the most vulnerable to burnout (and most in need of supportive supervision). In addition, burnout is more likely when the supervisor is perceived as being low in consideration (see Motivation, Job Commitment, and Leadership Behavior, earlier in this section).

c. Strategies for Preventing or Reducing Burnout: Generally, a supervisor can prevent or reduce burnout by decreasing stress on the worker which may involve removing him from the source of stress, reducing the impact of stressors, or helping the worker adjust to stress. Specific strategies for preventing and reducing burnout including the following (Borland, 1981; Kadushin & Harkness, 2002):

- Provide positive feedback.

- Arrange for a temporary reduction in caseload.

- Give the worker permission to prioritize his tasks so that some of his duties are temporarily reduced or suspended (e.g., some of his cases may need less frequent contact than others); give him permission to postpone a deadline; or help him sort out conflicting role responsibilities or performance objectives by, for example, officially giving top priority to one objective.

- Normalize and help the worker address negative feelings about a client – i.e., all feelings and thoughts are okay, as long as they're not exhibited in unprofessional behavior.

- Help the worker modify cognitions that produce stress (e.g., "If I make a wrong decision, something awful will happen to my client") by using reframing and cognitive restructuring. Provide the worker with needed perspective.

- Provide workers with a broader variety of job activities. ("Job enrichment" is a strategy that attempts to help workers find more meaning in the tasks assigned, and "job diversification" increases the variety of job-related tasks.)

- Encourage communication and develop a support system among staff and create opportunities for workers to share their concerns and feelings with peers.

- Encourage administrators to be supportive of staff.

- Promote the participation of staff members in decision-making.

- When hiring, make sure there is a good fit between the applicant and the job; provide realistic information about the job so that the applicant can make an informed decision about taking the job; and provide realistic information about the job to someone who's been hired so that he is less likely to be disappointed when he experiences the realities of the job. Underlying the use of anticipatory guidance and realistic job preview (RJP) is the assumption that disillusionment with the job is a primary cause of burnout and turnover – their purpose is to reduce unrealistic job expectations and, thereby, increase job satisfaction and commitment and lower turnover rates.

G. Evaluation/Performance Appraisal

Evaluation of a social worker's job performance is concerned with assessing his total functioning on the job over a specified period of time (e.g., 12 months), according to his individual skill level and job description. As noted earlier in this section, formal evaluation of a worker's job performance is an administrative task of supervision.

1. Objectives of Evaluation: Evaluation provides information to facilitate sound administrative decision-making on such issues as merit pay increases, promotion, suspension, reassignment, termination, and the like. Evaluation also contributes to a worker's professional development and improves his job performance by identifying his strengths and weaknesses. Ideally, an evaluation results in higher motivation and direction on the part of a worker. By achieving these objectives, evaluation ultimately improves the outcomes of agency service, thereby helping the agency meet accountability demands.

2. Formal Evaluation Conferences and Evaluation Statements: Whereas regular individual supervisory conferences focus on reviewing a current case from the worker's caseload, the formal evaluation conference focuses on reviewing the worker's entire caseload, including summing up the briefer assessments made in regular conferences.

The supervisor and worker prepare for an evaluation conference by reviewing a range of material (e.g., the agency's evaluation outline, the supervisor's notes, and the worker's reports, recordings, and time sheets) and formulating an initial appraisal of the worker's job performance. In the conference, the supervisor and worker then discuss their perceptions.

After discussion of the worker's performance, the supervisor writes a formal evaluation statement. The statement should (a) focus on modifiable elements of the worker's performance and (b) provide tentative suggestions for improvement, rather than final conclusions (i.e., the statement is presumed to reflect how the worker performs at the time, and it is expected that his performance will improve).

Additionally, the evaluation statement should be given to the worker so that he can read it and make comments. If the worker expresses any objections that the supervisor agrees with, the supervisor should amend the statement to reflect these; if the worker has objections that the supervisor doesn't accept, the worker has the right to ask that a record of his objections be placed in his file.

Administration has the ultimate responsibility for implementing the results of performance appraisals.

3. Evaluation Characteristics and Procedures: Desired characteristics and procedures for job performance evaluations in social work include the following:

- A supervisor should notify workers in advance of when evaluations will occur, what information and standards will be used, who will see the results, how the results will be used, etc.

- An evaluation should be job related and cover a specified period of time.

- An evaluation should cover both the quality of performance and the quantity of work output.

- An evaluation should be individualized and based on clearly specified, realistic, and achievable criteria that reflect the agency's standards.

- An evaluation should assess both strengths and weaknesses.

- An evaluation should not be based on personality factors, judgments of the worker as a person, the supervisor's personal standards, or political mechanisms.

- An evaluation should focus on recurrent patterns of behavior in job performance, not atypical, isolated examples of the worker's behavior.

- A supervisor should take into account special factors that may have affected the worker's performance, such as an unusually heavy caseload, numerous difficult cases, the unavailability of needed support services, or a period of low morale in the unit.

- An evaluation should distinguish a worker-related problem from an agency-related one. This requires the supervisor to be aware of current and recent organizational problems (e.g., staff shortage, new legislation affecting the agency) and to take these into account when judging a worker's performance.

- A supervisor should apply the same standards in the same way to all of her workers who have about the same education and experience. The same is true for different supervisors of different units of workers at the agency when the workers have similar backgrounds.

- An evaluation must be conducted and communicated as a mutual process in the context of a positive working relationship between the supervisor and worker.

- A supervisor should solicit a worker's reaction to the evaluation statement, and a worker's appropriate contributions to the evaluation should be part of the final evaluation report.

- An agency should have procedures that allow workers to appeal an evaluation, and a supervisor should encourage access to these procedures without making workers uncomfortable.

4. Sources of Information for an Evaluation: The supervisor needs to obtain valid and reliable information that reflects a worker's typical job performance. Sources of information available to the supervisor include (a) the worker's written records and verbal reports; (b) the worker's letters, reports, statistical forms, daily action logs, monthly performance records, etc.; (c) recordings of worker-client interactions; (d) observation of the worker from behind a one-way mirror, in BITE supervision, in joint interviews, in group supervisory meetings, in staff meetings, etc.; (e) peer and client evaluations of the worker's performance; and (f) client and organizational outcomes.

5. Evaluation Criteria: Ideally, staff should participate in establishing the evaluation criteria. This helps ensure the selection of appropriate criteria, improves workers' understanding of expectations associated with the evaluation, and increases workers' commitment to the evaluation.

a. Characteristics of Evaluation Criteria: A criterion is a standard against which a comparison can be made. Desired characteristics of evaluation criteria include the following:

- Evaluation criteria must represent significant aspects of the worker's performance.
- Taken together, evaluation criteria should cover the total job description.
- Evaluation criteria must be explicit and formulated so that they can be measured in objective terms.

b. Outcome Data vs. Second-Order Criteria: In social work, it is often difficult to define in precise terms the nature of effective performance, the abilities needed to perform effectively, and the outcomes that signify effective performance. It is also hard to define standards of productivity because social work has no standard "product" – the desired outcome of intervention is better psychosocial functioning by clients, and many factors affecting outcome cannot be controlled by the worker (Kadushin & Harkness, 2002).

Because of these difficulties, most agencies use second-order criteria to define the content of evaluations. The assumption underlying the use of these criteria is that, if a worker has the needed knowledge, exhibits appropriate professional behavior and attitudes, and follows prescribed procedures, then her clients will be helped. In other words, evaluations focus on process and procedures rather than on product or outcome. When reliable outcome data are available, however, they should be considered in an evaluation of a worker's performance.

6. Evaluation Instruments/Formats: Any performance evaluation instrument should be:

- valid (it evaluates what it is supposed to evaluate);
- relevant (what it evaluates is relevant to the job);
- reliable (it provides consistent evaluations across workers and across time);
- discriminating (it allows for clearly differentiated levels of performance);
- bias free (it maximizes objectivity and minimizes factors that may lead to subjectivity); and

- practical and relatively easy to use.

Examples of evaluation instruments or formats include the following:

Standardized check forms: Most agencies use standardized check forms as guides to evaluation, in part, because they require relatively little time to develop and use. They also encourage more standardization in the evaluation process and permit accurate comparisons between different workers or the same worker with herself at different times. Most check forms include space at the end so that the supervisor can provide a summary statement that clarifies and/or integrates her ratings.

Several kinds of rating scales are available for use on check forms, including, for example, a 5-point scale (e.g., excellent, above average, average, below average, poor). A major problem with rating scales is that their reliability and validity are threatened by rater biases (rater biases are reviewed later in this section).

Evaluation outlines: Evaluation outlines generally cover the job responsibilities of a specific group of workers at a particular agency. They help ensure that performance appraisals focus on workers' job performance. They are useful as discussion guides during evaluation conferences and result in narrative descriptions of workers' performance. Evaluation outlines can be impractical because they require extensive observation of the worker and take a long time to produce and read.

Behavior-anchored rating scales (BARS): BARS can provide valid and reliable measures of abstract dimensions of job performance (e.g., motivation), but, because they take a long time to develop, they are impractical to use in most agencies.

7. Evaluation Content Areas: The primary content areas typically included in comprehensive evaluation outlines for social work include the following (Kadushin & Harkness, 2002): (a) ability to establish and maintain meaningful, effective, appropriately professional relationships with client systems; (b) social work process (i.e., knowledge and skills, such as data-gathering skills, diagnostic skills, treatment/intervention skills, interviewing skills, recording skills); (c) orientation to agency administration (e.g., knowledge of, commitment to, identification with objectives, policies, and procedures); (d) relationship to and use of supervision; (e) staff and community relationships; (f) management of work requirements and workload; (g) professionally related attributes and attitudes (e.g., adequate self-awareness and capacity for self-evaluation, behaves in accordance with social work values and ethics); and (h) cultural competence.

Notice that these various content areas reflect cognitive criteria (knowledge, self-awareness, etc.), affective criteria (attitudes, etc.), and performance criteria (various skills).

8. Evaluation Biases/Errors: Most supervisors (and other raters) are not aware of when a bias is affecting their judgment (i.e., rating errors are usually unintentional). Overall the best way to improve rating accuracy is to provide raters with adequate training, and training is most effective when it focuses on identifying and distinguishing between different levels of performance rather than on avoiding rater biases. Examples of rating biases/errors include the following:

Central tendency bias: Central tendency refers to a supervisor's (or any other rater's) consistent use of only the middle (average) range of a rating scale. This may operate, for example, when a supervisor must evaluate a worker but doesn't have enough information about his performance.

Halo effect: The halo effect occurs when a supervisor's evaluation of a worker on one dimension of job performance affects her evaluation of that worker on other, unrelated dimensions. A halo effect can be either "positive" or "negative." The term "halo effect" is also used when a supervisor's evaluation of specific dimensions of a worker's performance is influenced by her overall opinion of the worker's performance.

Leniency bias: This bias occurs when a supervisor is reluctant to give workers negative evaluations – her evaluations are more positive than they should be given the workers' actual performance. When all ratings are skewed in the positive direction, evaluations are less useful for administrative decision-making.

Recency bias: This bias occurs when the supervisor fails to take into account a worker's total performance over the entire evaluation period because she is overly influenced by the worker's most recent performance or by dramatic, atypical events that occurred.

Negativity effect: When people are given both positive and negative information about someone, they tend to give the negative information more weight in forming their general impression of that person. This tendency may operate in supervisors who are evaluating workers.

Contrast bias: Rather than using an objective standard, a supervisor may evaluate a worker against other workers in the unit, and if, for example, the other workers are excellent performers, an average performer may be rated as worse than he is because he is being compared to his "excellent" peers. In other instances of this bias, a supervisor uses *herself* as the standard: She compares a worker's performance with her self-assessment of how she thinks she would have performed in a similar situation.

H. Miscellaneous Topics Related to Supervision

1. Supervision of Community Organizers: Supervision of workers who are community organizers differs from traditional supervision in several ways, including the following:

- Community organizers often work in small agencies with limited staff or are members of small units within large agencies. Consequently, their agency or unit may have no hierarchical structure that has supervisory personnel, and an administrator, rather than a supervisor, may assign and review their work.

- Some of the traditional functions of supervision are less important in community organizing, in part, because community organizers do their work in a more public setting than most other social workers (i.e., outside of an office). Because their work is more visible, some traditional supervisory processes, such as conferences to review cases, may not be necessary. Generally, the work of supervisors in community settings tends to be more task-oriented.

- Because community organizers generally reject traditional bureaucratic structures and work away from their agencies (in the field), they are subject to pressures from many different groups. Therefore, an important task in supervising these workers is monitoring their loyalty to the agency, including their accountability to administration (e.g., the supervisor has to make sure that the workers don't commit the agency to activities or policies it can't support).

2. Supervision and Consultation Compared: The primary differences between supervision and consultation include the following:

- A supervisor is responsible for identifying a worker's problems. A consultant, by contrast, is hired after a problem has been identified — it is up to the consultee (or someone with authority over the consultee) to identify the problem and then seek the consultant's help.

- Supervision has administrative, educational, and supportive functions. Consultation only has an educational (problem-solving) function.

- A supervisor is responsible for a worker's overall job performance and professional development. A consultant focuses on just one work-related problem.

- Two important sources of a supervisor's power (i.e., her ability to implement her authority) are (a) the agency's administrative structure, which delegates authority to the supervisor, and (b) the worker, who accepts as legitimate his supervisor's entitlement to this authority. A supervisor has the authority to, among other things, enforce a worker's adherence to agency procedures and evaluate a worker's on-the-job performance. By contrast, a consultant's authority stems from her expertise and ability to persuade a consultee. The consultant has no administrative authority over a worker (consultee), and a worker is free to reject the consultant's suggestions.

3. Supervision vs. Psychotherapy: A supervisor's efforts to help workers develop self-awareness and modify certain feelings, behaviors, and attitudes have some resemblance to the work done with clients in psychotherapy. Therefore, supervisors must always keep in mind the possible risks and conflicts associated with **dual relationships** – a supervisor must avoid serving as psychotherapist to a worker she is supervising.

Some of the key differences between educational supervision and therapy include the following (Kadushin & Harkness, 2002):

- A supervisor is concerned with a worker's professional activities and has no authority to intrude into a worker's personal life.

- A worker's behaviors, feelings, and personal attitudes are a legitimate topic for supervision *only* if they interfere with the worker's performance of professional tasks.

- A worker can't choose his supervisor or terminate the relationship with his supervisor; a psychotherapy client can usually voluntarily select his therapist and is usually free to terminate therapy when he wants to.

Appendix I: Summary of the NASW Code of Ethics

This appendix paraphrases the values, principles, and standards contained in the NASW Code of Ethics.

The NASW Code of Ethics (NASW, 2017)

Preamble

The Preamble to the NASW Code of Ethics includes the following key points.

1. Your primary mission as a professional social worker is "to enhance human well-being and help meet the basic human needs of all people, with particular attention to the needs and empowerment of people who are vulnerable, oppressed, and living in poverty."

2. Your primary mission is based on a set of core values: service; social justice; dignity and worth of the person; importance of human relationships; integrity; and competence. These values also serve as the basis for the principles contained in the Code of Ethics.

The idea is that as a social worker, you have embraced these values and will use them to guide your professional work. In addition, however, you must also apply these values and principles within the "context and complexity of the human experience."

3. A fundamental aspect of your work is "a focus on individual well-being in a social context and the well-being of society."

4. As a social worker, your duties and objectives include the following:

   a. "Promoting social justice and social change with and on behalf of clients." Your "clients" may include individuals, families, groups, organizations, and communities.

   b. Remaining "sensitive to ethnic and cultural diversity" and working to "end discrimination, oppression, poverty, and other forms of social injustice."

   c. "Enhancing the capacity of people to address their own needs" and "promoting the responsiveness of organizations, communities, and other social institutions to individuals' needs and social problems."

Ethical Principles

According to NASW, the following broad principles are intended to "set forth ideals to which all social workers should aspire."

1. VALUE: Service

Ethical Principle: As a social worker, your primary goal is "to help people in need and to address social problems."

In order to abide by this principle, you should place service to others above your own self-interest. In addition, the Code of Ethics encourages you to provide pro bono services. (Pro bono services are professional services for which you expect no significant payment.)

2. VALUE: Social Justice

Ethical Principle: You "challenge social injustice."

In order to follow this principle, you should work to bring about social change with and on behalf of individuals and groups, especially those who are vulnerable and oppressed. Important goals of your activities in this area include the following:

> 1. Increasing sensitivity to and knowledge about oppression and ethnic and cultural diversity.
>
> 2. Improving access to needed information, services, and resources.
>
> 3. Promoting equal opportunity and the chance for all individuals to participate in decision making in a meaningful way.

3. VALUE: Dignity and Worth of the Person

Ethical Principle: You "respect the inherent dignity and worth of the person."

In order to abide by this principle, you should:

> 1. Treat each person in a compassionate and respectful way, which includes taking into account cultural and ethnic differences.
>
> 2. Promote your clients' self-determination whenever it is socially responsible to do so.
>
> 3. Work to improve your clients' capacity and opportunity to change and to meet their own needs.
>
> 4. Attempt to settle conflicts between your clients' interests and the interests of the broader society. When seeking a resolution, you should act in a socially responsible way and ensure that your behavior is consistent with social work values and the Code of Ethics.

4. VALUE: Importance of Human Relationships

Ethical Principle: You "recognize the central importance of human relationships."

In order to follow this principle, you should:

> 1. Understand that relationships are an important means of achieving change and thus work to strengthen the relationships of all of the clients you serve as a means of promoting, restoring, maintaining, and increasing their well-being.
>
> 2. Engage your clients and others who receive your services as partners in the helping process.

5. VALUE: Integrity

Ethical Principle: You "behave in a trustworthy manner."

In order to abide by this principle, you should:

1. Remain cognizant of the mission, values, ethical principles, and ethical standards of your profession and always conduct your professional work in a manner that is consistent with them.

2. Act honestly and responsibly.

3. Promote ethical practices by the organizations with which you are associated.

6. VALUE: Competence

Ethical Principle: You "practice within [your] areas of competence and develop and enhance [your] professional expertise."

In order to follow this principle, you should:

1. Work to increase your own professional knowledge and skills and apply them in your practice.

2. Contribute to the knowledge base of the social work profession.

Ethical Standards

NASW divides the ethical standards into six parts, and each part contains numerous sections – e.g., section (a), section (b). In presenting this section of the Code of Ethics, we have also *numbered* the requirements in list form, in order to facilitate your review. These numbers (1, 2, 3, etc.) do not appear in the NASW Code of Ethics.

1. ETHICAL RESPONSIBILITIES TO CLIENTS

1.01 COMMITMENT TO CLIENTS

1. Your most important consideration is the best interests of your clients.

2. Your primary duty is to advance the well-being of your clients.

3. On limited occasions, your obligations to society or a specific legal requirement may override this general responsibility (for example, when you are required by law to report that a child has been abused).

4. You should inform your clients about the situations described in #3.

1.02 SELF-DETERMINATION

1. You should respect and promote the right of your clients to self-determination.

2. You should help your clients determine and clarify their goals.

3. You may limit a client's right to self-determination when, based on your professional judgment, you conclude that his or her actions or potential actions pose a "serious, foreseeable, and imminent" risk to self or others.

1.03 INFORMED CONSENT

Section (a):

1. You should provide your services to clients only within the context of a professional relationship.

2. When appropriate, you must obtain a valid informed consent from a client in order to provide your services.

3. As part of obtaining an informed consent, you must tell a client about:

   a. the purpose of your services,

   b. the risks related to these services,

   c. the limits to these services due to a third-party payer's requirements,

   d. relevant costs,

   e. reasonable alternatives,

   f. the client's right to refuse or withdraw consent, and

   g. the time-frame covered by the consent.

4. When informing a client about the matters in #3, you must use clear and understandable language and give the client an opportunity to ask questions.

Section (b):

5. If a client is illiterate or has difficulty understanding the primary language used in your practice setting, you should take steps to ensure that the client obtains as much understanding as possible about the available services. For example, you can provide the client with a detailed verbal explanation. If possible, you should bring in a qualified interpreter or translator.

Section (c):

6. If a client lacks the capacity to provide informed consent, you must attempt to protect the client's interests.

7. You should take reasonable steps to increase such a client's ability to give informed consent for himself or herself.

   a. You should provide the client with an explanation of the services to the extent possible, based on his or her ability to understand the information.

   b. You should seek to obtain consent from an appropriate third party.

   c. You should take steps to ensure that the third party acts in a manner consistent with the client's wishes and interests.

Section (d):

8. If a client is receiving your services involuntarily, you should inform the client about the nature and extent of the services and his or her right to refuse the services.

Section (e):

9. You should discuss with clients the your policies concerning the use of technology in the provision of professional services.

Section (f):

10. If you use technology to provide social work services you should obtain informed consent from the individuals using these services during the initial screening or interview and prior to initiating services.

11. You should assess clients' capacity to provide informed consent and, when using technology to communicate, verify the identity and location of clients.

Section (g):

12. If you use technology to provide social work services you should assess the clients' suitability and capacity for electronic and remote services.

13. You should consider the clients' intellectual, emotional, and physical ability to use technology to receive services and ability to understand the potential benefits, risks, and limitations of such services. If clients do not wish to use services provided through technology, you should help them identify alternate methods of service.

Section (h):

14. You should obtain clients' informed consent before making audio or video recordings of clients or permitting observation of service provision by a third party.

Section (i):

15. You should obtain client consent before conducting an electronic search on the client. Exceptions may arise when the search is for purposes of protecting the client or others from serious, foreseeable, and imminent harm, or for other compelling professional reasons.

1.04 COMPETENCE

Section (a):

1. You should provide services only within the bounds of your education, training, license/certification, consultation received, supervised experience, or other relevant professional experience.

2. You should represent yourself as competent only within the bounds of your education, training, license/certification, consultation received, supervised experience, or other relevant professional experience.

Section (b):

3. If you wish to provide services in substantive areas that are new to you or apply intervention techniques or approaches that are new to you, you should engage in appropriate study, training, consultation, and supervision beforehand.

4. You must ensure that the individuals who prepare you to use a new intervention or technique are competent in the intervention or technique.

Section (c):

5. If there are no generally recognized standards for a new area of practice, you must safeguard the competence of your work and protect your clients from harm by:

   a. using careful judgment, and

   b. taking responsible steps, such as engaging in appropriate education, research, training, consultation, and supervision.

Section (d):

6. If you use technology in the provision of social work services you should ensure that you have the necessary knowledge and skills to provide such services in a competent manner. This includes an understanding of the special communication challenges when using technology and the ability to implement strategies to address these challenges.

Section (e):

7. If you use technology in providing social work services you should comply with the laws governing technology and social work practice in the jurisdiction in which they are regulated and located and, as applicable, in the jurisdiction in which the client is located.

1.05 CULTURAL AWARENESS AND SOCIAL DIVERSITY

Section (a):

1. You should understand culture and the role it plays in human behavior and society.

2. You should recognize that strengths exist in all cultures.

Section (b):

3. You should have knowledge about your clients' cultures.

4. You should be capable of providing services that are sensitive to people's cultures and to differences among people and cultural groups.

Section (c):

5. You should get education about and attempt to understand the nature of social diversity and oppression related to race, ethnicity, national origin, color, sex, sexual orientation, gender identity or expression, age, marital status, political belief, religion, immigration status, and mental or physical ability.

Section (d):

6. If you provide electronic social work services you should be aware of cultural and socioeconomic differences among clients and how they may use electronic technology.

7. You should assess cultural, environmental, economic, mental or physical ability, linguistic, and other issues that may affect the delivery or use of these services.

1.06 CONFLICTS OF INTEREST

Section (a):

1. You should be alert to and avoid conflicts of interest that interfere with your exercise of professional discretion and objective judgment.

2. You should inform your clients when a real or potential conflict of interest arises.

3. If such a conflict arises or is likely to arise, you should take reasonable steps to resolve the conflict in a way that considers the clients' interests first and protects their interests to the greatest extent possible.

4. Sometimes, in order to protect a client's interests when there is conflict of interest, you will need to terminate the professional relationship.

5. If you must terminate a professional relationship due to a conflict of interest, you must provide for proper referral of the client.

Section (b):

6. You should not take unfair advantage of any professional relationship you have or exploit anyone to further your own personal, religious, political, or business interests.

Section (c):

7. You should not engage in dual or multiple relationships with a client or former client when there is a risk of exploitation or potential harm to the client.

8. If a dual or multiple relationship is unavoidable, you should take steps to protect the client.

9. In the situation described in #8, you are responsible for setting clear, appropriate, and culturally sensitive boundaries.

Section (d):

10. When providing services to two or more people who have a relationship with each other (e.g., couples, family members), you should clarify with all parties:

   a. which individuals you will view as the "client," and

   b. the nature of your professional responsibilities to each person receiving your services.

11. If you anticipate a conflict of interest among the individuals receiving your services or anticipate having to perform in potentially conflicting roles (e.g., you may be asked to testify in a child custody dispute or the clients may initiate a divorce proceeding), you should clarify your role with all of the individuals involved.

12. If this type of conflict of interest arises (see #11), you should take appropriate steps to minimize it.

Section (e):

13. You should avoid communication with clients using technology (such as social networking sites, online chat, e-mail, text messages, telephone, and video) for personal or non-work-related purposes.

Section (f):

14. You should be aware that posting personal information on professional Web sites or other media might cause boundary confusion, inappropriate dual relationships, or harm to clients.

Section (g):

15. You should be aware that personal affiliations may increase the likelihood that clients may discover your presence on Web sites, social media, and other forms of technology.

16. You should be aware that involvement in electronic communication with groups based on race, ethnicity, language, sexual orientation, gender identity or expression, mental or physical ability, religion, immigration status, and other personal affiliations may affect your ability to work effectively with particular clients.

Section (h):

17. You should avoid accepting requests from or engaging in personal relationships with clients on social networking sites or other electronic media to prevent boundary confusion, inappropriate dual relationships, or harm to clients.

1.07 PRIVACY AND CONFIDENTIALITY

Section (a):

1. You should respect your clients' rights to privacy.

2. You should not solicit private information from a client except for compelling professional reasons.

3. After you obtain private information, the standards of confidentiality apply.

Section (b):

4. You can disclose confidential information, when appropriate, with valid consent from a client or from a person legally authorized to consent on behalf of a client.

Section (c):

5. In general, you should protect the confidentiality of all information you obtain in the course of your professional service.

6. An exception to #5 occurs when there is a "compelling professional reason" to disclose the information; i.e., the assumption that you will keep information confidential does not apply when:

   a. you need to disclose certain information to prevent serious, foreseeable, and imminent harm to a client or others, or

   b. laws or regulations require you to disclose certain information without a client's consent.

7. In the situations described in #6, you should disclose the least amount of confidential information necessary to achieve your intended purpose. In other words, you should disclose only information that is directly relevant to the purpose for which you are making the disclosure.

Section (d):

8. To the extent possible, you should inform a client about the disclosure of confidential information and the possible consequences.

9. When feasible, you should inform the client of the matters described in #8 before you make the disclosure.

10. The requirements in #8 and #9 apply whenever you disclose confidential information based on a legal requirement or a client's consent.

Section (e):

11. You should explain to your clients and other interested parties the nature of confidentiality.

12. You should discuss with clients the limitations to their right of confidentiality. In particular, you should discuss:

a. the circumstances when confidential information may be requested, and

b. when disclosure of confidential information may be required by law.

13. You should have this discussion (see #11 and #12) with a client as soon as possible in the relationship and then as needed during the course of the relationship.

Section (f):

14. When you provide counseling services to families, couples, or groups, you should try to obtain an agreement from and among all of the clients involved in the counseling regarding each one's right to confidentiality and each one's obligation to maintain the confidentiality of information shared by the others. This agreement should include consideration of whether confidential information may be exchanged in person or electronically.

15. You should tell participants in family, couples, or group counseling that you cannot guarantee that the others involved in the counseling will abide by the confidentiality agreement (see #14).

Section (g):

16. When you perform family, couples, or group counseling, you should inform the clients of your own, your employer's, and your agency's policy regarding whether or not and when you will disclose confidential information among the clients involved in the counseling.

Section (h):

17. You should not disclose confidential information to third-party payers unless the client has authorized you to do so.

Section (i):

18. You should not talk about confidential information, electronically or in person, in any setting unless privacy can be guaranteed. For example, you should not discuss confidential information in public or semi-public areas (e.g., hallways, waiting rooms, restaurants).

Section (j):

19. To the degree permitted by law, you should protect the confidentiality of your clients during legal proceedings.

20. If a legally authorized body, such as a court of law, orders you to disclose confidential or privileged information without a client's consent and you believe that such disclosure could result in harm to the client, you should:

a. ask the court to withdraw the order,

b. try to limit the order as narrowly as possible, or

c. keep the relevant records under seal, where they are unavailable for public inspection.

Section (k):

21. You should protect the confidentiality of your clients when responding to requests from members of the media.

Section (l):

22. You should protect the confidentiality of your clients' written and electronic records and other sensitive information.

23. You should take reasonable steps to make sure that clients' records are stored in a secure place and are not available to others who are not authorized to obtain or read them.

Section (m):

24. You should take reasonable steps to protect the confidentiality of electronic communications, including information provided to clients or third parties.

25. You should use applicable safeguards (such as encryption, firewalls, and passwords) when using electronic communications such as e-mail, online posts, online chat sessions, mobile communication, and text messages.

Section (n):

26. You should develop and disclose policies and procedures for notifying clients of any breach of confidential information in a timely manner.

Section (o):

27. In the event of unauthorized access to client records or information, including any unauthorized access to your electronic communication or storage systems, you should inform clients of such disclosures, consistent with applicable laws and professional standards.

Section (p):

28. You should develop and inform clients about their policies, consistent with prevailing social work ethical standards, on the use of electronic technology, including Internet-based search engines, to gather information about clients.

Section (q):

29. You should avoid searching or gathering client information electronically unless there are compelling professional reasons, and when appropriate, with the client's informed consent.

Section (r):

30. You should avoid posting any identifying or confidential information about clients on professional Web sites or other forms of social media.

Section (s):

31. You should transfer or dispose of clients' records in a manner that protects clients' confidentiality and is consistent with applicable laws governing records and social work licensure.

Section (t):

32. You should take reasonable precautions to protect client confidentiality in the event of the social worker's termination of practice, incapacitation, or death.

Section (u):

33. You should not disclose identifying information when discussing clients for teaching or training purposes unless the client has consented to disclosure of confidential information.

Section (v):

34. You should not disclose identifying information when discussing clients with consultants unless the client has consented to disclosure of confidential information or there is a compelling need for such disclosure.

Section (w):

35. You should protect the confidentiality of deceased clients consistent with the preceding standards.

1.08 ACCESS TO RECORDS

Section (a):

1. You should provide your clients with reasonable access to records concerning them.

2. If you are concerned that such access will result in misunderstanding or serious harm to the client, you should:

   a. provide the client with help in interpreting the records, and

   b. consult with the client about the records.

3. You should limit a client's access to his or her records, or part of the records, only in exceptional circumstances, as when there is compelling evidence that seeing certain information in the record would result in serious harm to the client.

4. If you limit a client's access to all or part of his or her records, you should document in the client's file:

   a. the client's request for the records, and

   b. the reasons why you withheld all or part of the records from the client.

Section (b):

5. When providing clients with access to their records, you should take steps to protect the confidentiality of other people identified or discussed in the records.

1.09 SEXUAL RELATIONSHIPS

Section (a):

1. You should never, under any circumstances, engage in sexual activity, inappropriate sexual communications through the use of technology or in person, or sexual contact with a current client.

2. The prohibition in #1 applies whether sexual contact with a current client is consensual or forced.

Section (b):

3. You should not engage in sexual contact with a client's relatives or other people with whom the client has a close personal relationship when there is a risk of exploitation or

harm to the client. Sexual activity or sexual contact with these individuals can harm the client and make it difficult for you and the client to maintain appropriate professional boundaries.

4. In the situation described in #3, you bear the full burden for setting clear, appropriate, and culturally sensitive boundaries.

Section (c):

5. You should not engage in sexual activity or sexual contact with a former client because doing so may harm the client.

6. If you become sexually involved with a former client, or want to claim that there is exception to this standard because of unusual circumstances, you bear the full burden of proving that the former client has not been exploited, coerced, or manipulated, either intentionally or unintentionally.

Section (d):

7. You should not provide clinical services to anyone with whom you have had a prior sexual relationship because doing so has the potential of harming this person and is likely to make it difficult for you and this person to maintain appropriate professional boundaries.

1.10 PHYSICAL CONTACT

1. You should not engage in physical contact with a client (e.g., cradling) if there is a chance that such contact will result in psychological harm to the client.

2. If you engage in appropriate physical contact with a client, you should set clear, appropriate, and culturally sensitive professional boundaries that govern the contact.

1.11 SEXUAL HARASSMENT

1. You should not sexually harass clients. Sexual harassment includes sexual advances; sexual solicitation; requests for sexual favors; and other verbal, written, electronic, or physical contact of a sexual nature.

1.12 DEROGATORY LANGUAGE

1. You should not use derogatory language in your written, verbal, or electronic communications to or about clients.

2. You should use accurate and respectful language in all communications to and about clients.

1.13 PAYMENT FOR SERVICES

Section (a):

1. When setting a fee for your services, you should make sure that it is fair, reasonable, and consistent with the services you perform.

2. When setting a fee for your services, you should give consideration to a client's ability to pay.

Section (b):

3. Ordinarily, you should avoid accepting goods or services from your clients as payment for professional services. Such bartering arrangements, especially those involving your services, may result in conflicts of interest, exploitation, and inappropriate boundaries in your relationship with a client.

4. In very limited circumstances, you can explore and may engage in bartering with a client; i.e., you may do so when you can demonstrate that the bartering arrangement:

   a. is an accepted practice among professionals in your community,

   b. is viewed as essential for the provision of services,

   c. has been negotiated without coercion, and

   d. has been entered into at the request of the client and with the client's informed consent.

5. If you accept goods or services from a client as payment for your professional services, you bear the full burden of demonstrating that this arrangement will not harm the client or the professional relationship.

Section (c):

6. You should not ask for a private fee or other remuneration when providing services to a client who is entitled to such available services through your employer or agency.

1.14 CLIENTS WHO LACK DECISION-MAKING CAPACITY

1. When you act on behalf of a client who lacks the capacity to make an informed decision, you should take reasonable steps to protect the interests and rights of this client.

1.15 INTERRUPTION OF SERVICES

1. You should make reasonable efforts to ensure continuity of services in the event that services are interrupted by factors such as unavailability, disruptions in electronic communication, relocation, illness, mental or physical ability, or death.

1.16 REFERRAL FOR SERVICES

Section (a):

1. You should refer clients to other professionals when the other professionals' specialized knowledge or expertise is needed to serve clients fully or when you believe that they are not being effective or making reasonable progress with clients and that other services are required.

Section (b):

1. If you refer clients to other professionals you should take appropriate steps to facilitate an orderly transfer of responsibility.

2. If you refer clients to other professionals you should disclose, with clients' consent, all pertinent information to the new service providers.

Section (c):

1. You are prohibited from giving or receiving payment for a referral when no professional service is provided by the referring social worker.

1.17 TERMINATION OF SERVICES

Section (a):

1. You should terminate your services to a client and your professional relationship with the client when your services and the relationship are no longer needed or no longer serve the client's needs or interests.

Section (b):

2. You should take reasonable steps to avoid abandoning a client who still needs your services.

3. You should withdraw your services abruptly only under extraordinary circumstances, giving due consideration to all aspects of the situation and taking care to minimize possible negative effects.

4. If you must terminate your services to a client abruptly, you should, when necessary, assist in making appropriate arrangements for alternative services for the client.

Section (c):

5. If you work in a fee-for-service setting, you may terminate your services to a client who is not paying his or her overdue balance if the following conditions are met:

   a. the financial contractual arrangements have been made clear to the client,

   b. the client is not an imminent danger to self or others, and

   c. you have addressed and discussed the clinical and other consequences of nonpayment with the client.

Section (d):

6. You should not terminate your services to a client for the purposes of pursuing a social, financial, or sexual relationship with the client.

Section (e):

7. If you anticipate the termination or interruption of your services to a client, you should:

   a. inform the client promptly, and

   b. seek the transfer, referral, or continuation of services, in accordance with the client's needs and preferences.

Section (f):

8. If you are leaving an employment setting, you should tell your clients about:

   a. appropriate options for the continuation of services, and

   b. the risks and benefits associated with their options.

2. ETHICAL RESPONSIBILITIES TO COLLEAGUES

2.01 RESPECT

Section (a):

1. You should treat your colleagues with respect.

2. You should represent accurately and fairly the qualifications, views, and obligations of your colleagues.

Section (b):

3. You should avoid criticizing your colleagues in unwarranted and negative ways when communicating with clients or other professionals.

4. Such criticism (see #3) may include demeaning comments that refer to a colleague's level of competence or individual characteristics such as race, ethnicity, national origin, color, sex, sexual orientation, gender identity or expression, age, marital status, political belief, religion, immigration status, and mental or physical ability.

Section (c):

5. You should cooperate with social work colleagues and colleagues from other professions when such cooperation serves the well-being of clients.

2.02 CONFIDENTIALITY

1. You should respect confidential information shared by colleagues in the course of their professional relationships and transactions.

2. You should make sure colleagues understand your obligation to respect confidentiality and any exceptions related to it.

2.03 INTERDISCIPLINARY COLLABORATION

Section (a):

1. When serving as a member of an interdisciplinary team, you should:

    a. take part in and contribute to decisions that impact the well-being of clients, and

    b. draw on the perspectives, values, and experiences of the social work profession.

2. The ethical and professional obligations of the interdisciplinary team as a whole and of each member should be clearly established.

Section (b):

3. If an interdisciplinary team decision raises ethical concerns, you should attempt to resolve the dispute through appropriate channels.

4. If the dispute cannot be resolved (see #3), you should pursue other means to address your concerns.

5. The means you pursue (see #4), as well as the resolution you choose, should be consistent with the client's well-being.

2.04 DISPUTES INVOLVING COLLEAGUES

Section (a):

1. You should not take advantage of a disagreement between a colleague and an employer to obtain a position or otherwise advance your own interests.

Section (b):

2. You should not exploit your clients in a disagreement with colleagues.

3. You should not involve your clients in any inappropriate discussion of a conflict between you and a colleague.

2.05 CONSULTATION

Section (a):

1. You should seek the advice and counsel of colleagues whenever such consultation is in the best interests of a client.

Section (b):

2. You should stay informed of your colleagues' areas of expertise and competence.

3. You should seek consultation only from colleagues who have demonstrated knowledge, expertise, and competence related to the subject of the consultation.

Section (c):

4. When consulting with a colleague about a client, you should disclose the least amount of information necessary to accomplish the purpose (or purposes) of the consultation.

2.06 SEXUAL RELATIONSHIPS

Section (a):

1. When you function as a supervisor or educator, you should not engage in sexual activities or contact (including verbal, written, electronic, or physical contact) with your supervisees, students, trainees, or other colleagues over whom you have professional authority.

Section (b):

2. You should avoid having a sexual relationship with a colleague when there is the potential for a conflict of interest.

3. If you do become involved in or anticipate becoming involved in a sexual relationship with a colleague, you have an obligation to transfer professional responsibilities, when necessary, to avoid a conflict of interest.

2.07 SEXUAL HARASSMENT

1. You should not sexually harass supervisees, students, trainees, or colleagues.

2. Sexual harassment includes sexual advances; sexual solicitation; requests for sexual favors; and other verbal, written, electronic, or physical contact of a sexual nature.

2.08 IMPAIRMENT OF COLLEAGUES

Section (a):

1. When you acquire direct knowledge of a social work colleague's impairment due to personal problems, psychological distress, substance abuse, or mental health difficulties, and the impairment is interfering with the colleague's practice effectiveness, you should consult with that colleague, if feasible, and help him or her take remedial action.

Section (b):

2. When you believe that a social work colleague's impairment is interfering with his or her practice effectiveness and that the colleague has not taken adequate steps to address

the impairment, you should take action through appropriate channels developed by your employer, the agency, NASW, a licensing or regulatory body, and other professional organizations.

2.09 INCOMPETENCE OF COLLEAGUES

Section (a):

1. When you have direct knowledge of a social work colleague's incompetence, you should consult with that colleague, if feasible, and help the colleague take remedial action.

Section (b):

2. When you believe that a social work colleague is incompetent and that the colleague has not taken adequate steps to address the incompetence, you should take action through appropriate channels developed by your employer, the agency, NASW, a licensing or regulatory body, and other professional organizations.

2.10 UNETHICAL CONDUCT OF COLLEAGUES

Section (a):

1. You should take adequate steps to discourage, prevent, expose, and correct the unethical conduct of your colleagues, including unethical conduct using technology.

Section (b):

2. You should know about established policies and procedures for handling concerns about a colleague's unethical behavior.

3. You should be familiar with national, state, and local procedures for handling ethical complaints; i.e., policies and procedures created by NASW, licensing and regulatory bodies, employers, agencies, and other professional organizations.

Section (c):

4. When you believe that a colleague has acted unethically, you should seek resolution by discussing your concerns with the colleague when feasible and when the discussion is likely to be productive.

Section (d):

5. When you believe that a colleague has acted unethically, if necessary (e.g., if a discussion is not likely to be productive), you should take action through appropriate formal channels; e.g., contacting a state licensing board or regulatory body, the NASW Ethics Committee, or other professional ethics committee.

Section (e):

6. You should defend and help colleagues who have been unfairly charged with unethical conduct.

3. ETHICAL RESPONSIBILITIES IN PRACTICE SETTINGS

3.01 SUPERVISION AND CONSULTATION

If you provide supervision or consultation, whether in-person or remotely:

1. You should have the necessary knowledge and skill to supervise or consult appropriately (section a).

2. You should provide supervision or consultation only within your areas of knowledge and competence (section a).

3. You are responsible for setting clear, appropriate, and culturally sensitive boundaries (section b).

4. As a supervisor, you should not engage in any dual or multiple relationships with a supervisee when there is a risk of exploitation of or potential harm to the supervisee, including dual relationships that may arise while using social networking sites or other electronic media (section c).

5. As a supervisor, you should evaluate your supervisees' performance in a manner that is fair and respectful (section d).

3.02 EDUCATION AND TRAINING

If you function as an educator, field instructor for students, or trainer:

1. You should provide instruction only within your areas of knowledge and competence (section a).

2. Your instruction should be based on the most current information and knowledge available in the profession (section a).

3. As an educator or field instructor, you should evaluate your students' performance in a manner that is fair and respectful (section b).

4. As an educator or field instructor, you should take reasonable steps to make sure that clients are routinely informed when services are being provided to them by students (section c).

5. As an educator or field instructor for students, you should not engage in any dual or multiple relationships with a student when there is a risk of exploitation of or potential harm to the student (section d).

6. As an educator or field instructor, you are responsible for setting clear, appropriate, and culturally sensitive boundaries (section d).

7. If you function as an educator or field instructors for students you should not engage in any dual or multiple relationships with students in which there is a risk of exploitation or potential harm to the student, including dual relationships that may arise while using social networking sites or other electronic media.

3.03 PERFORMANCE EVALUATION

If you have responsibility for evaluating the performance of others:

1. You should discharge this responsibility in a fair and considerate way, and on the basis of clearly stated criteria.

3.04 CLIENT RECORDS

Section (a):

1. You should take reasonable steps to make sure that documentation in electronic and paper records is accurate and reflects the services provided.

Section (b):

2. You should include adequate and timely documentation in records to facilitate the delivery of services and guarantee the continuity of services provided to clients in the future.

Section (c):

3. Your documentation should protect clients' privacy to the degree that is possible and appropriate.

4. Your documentation should include only information that is directly relevant to the delivery of services.

Section (d):

5. You should store records after the termination of services in a way that guarantees reasonable access in the future.

6. You should maintain your records for the number of years required by relevant laws, agency policies, and contracts.

3.05 BILLING

1. You should create and maintain billing practices that accurately reflect the nature and extent of services provided and identify who provided the service in the practice setting.

3.06 CLIENT TRANSFER

Section (a):

1. If a potential client who is receiving services from another agency or colleague contacts you for services, you should carefully consider the client's needs before agreeing to provide your services.

2. To minimize possible conflict and confusion, you should discuss with the potential client (see #1):

   a. the nature of his or her current relationship with the other service provider, and

   b. the implications, including possible risks or benefits, of entering into a professional relationship with you.

Section (b):

3. If a new client has been served by another agency or colleague, you should discuss with the client whether consultation with the previous service provider is in the client's best interests.

3.07 ADMINISTRATION

If you function as a social work administrator:

1. You should advocate within and outside your agency for adequate resources to meet your clients' needs (section a).

2. You should advocate for resource allocation procedures that are open and impartial (section b).

3. When not all clients' needs can be met, an allocation procedure should be developed that is nondiscriminatory and based on appropriate and consistently applied principles (section b).

4. You should take reasonable steps to make sure that adequate agency or organizational resources are available to provide appropriate staff supervision (section c).

5. You should take reasonable steps to make sure that the working environment for which you are responsible is consistent with and encourages compliance with the NASW Code of Ethics (section d).

6. You should take reasonable steps to eliminate any conditions in your organization that violate, interfere with, or discourage compliance with the NASW Code of Ethics (section d).

3.08 CONTINUING EDUCATION AND STAFF DEVELOPMENT

Continuing education and staff development should deal with current knowledge and new developments related to social work practice and ethics. If you function as a supervisor or social work administrator:

1. You should take reasonable steps to provide or arrange for continuing education and staff development for all staff for whom you are responsible.

3.09 COMMITMENT TO EMPLOYERS

Section (a):

1. In general, you should meet all of the commitments you make to your employer and employing organization.

Section (b):

2. You should work to improve your employing agency's policies and procedures and the efficiency and effectiveness of its services.

Section (c):

3. You should take reasonable steps to ensure that your employer is aware of your ethical obligations (as defined in this Code of Ethics) and the implications of these obligations for your practice as a social worker.

Section (d):

4. You should not allow your employing organization's policies, procedures, regulations, or administrative orders to interfere with your ethical practice of social work.

5. You should take reasonable steps to ensure that your employing organization's practices are consistent with the NASW Code of Ethics.

Section (e):

6. You should act to prevent and end discrimination in your employing organization's work assignments, as well as its employment policies and practices.

Section (f):

7. You should accept employment or arrange student field placements only in organizations that apply fair personnel practices.

Section (g):

   8. You should be a prudent custodian of the resources of your employing organization; i.e., you should conserve funds where appropriate and never misuse funds or use them for purposes for which they were not intended.

3.10 LABOR-MANAGEMENT DISPUTES

Section (a):

   1. You are permitted to engage in organized action, including the creation of and participation in a labor union, to improve services to clients and working conditions.

Section (b):

   2. When involved in labor-management disputes, job actions, or labor strikes, your actions should be guided by your profession's values, ethical principles, and ethical standards.

   3. During an actual or threatened labor strike or job action, there will be reasonable differences of opinion among social workers related to their fundamental obligation as professionals. Therefore, you should carefully consider all relevant issues and their possible effect on clients before deciding on a course of action.

4. ETHICAL RESPONSIBILITIES AS PROFESSIONALS

4.01 COMPETENCE

Section (a):

   1. You should accept responsibility or employment only on the basis of existing competence or the intention to acquire the necessary competence.

Section (b):

   2. You should seek to become and remain proficient in your professional practice and the performance of your professional functions.

   3. You should critically evaluate and stay current with new knowledge related to social work.

   4. You should routinely review the professional literature.

   5. You should participate in continuing education related to social work practice and social work ethics.

Section (c):

   6. You should base your practice on recognized knowledge, including empirically based knowledge, related to social work and social work ethics.

4.02 DISCRIMINATION

   1. You should not practice, condone, facilitate, or collaborate with any form of discrimination based on race, ethnicity, national origin, color, sex, sexual orientation, gender identity or expression, age, marital status, political belief, religion, immigration status, or mental or physical ability.

4.03 PRIVATE CONDUCT

1. You should not allow your private conduct to interfere with your ability to fulfill your professional responsibilities.

4.04 DISHONESTY, FRAUD, AND DECEPTION

1. You should not participate in, condone, or be associated with dishonesty, fraud, or deception.

4.05 IMPAIRMENT

Section (a):

1. You should not allow your personal problems, psychological distress, legal problems, substance abuse, or mental health difficulties to interfere with your professional performance and judgment or to threaten the best interests of persons for whom you have a professional responsibility.

Section (b):

2. If your personal problems, psychological distress, legal problems, substance abuse, or mental health difficulties interfere with your professional performance and judgment, you should:

   a. immediately seek consultation, and

   b. take appropriate remedial action by getting professional help, adjusting your workload, terminating your practice, or taking any other steps necessary to protect your clients and others.

4.06 MISREPRESENTATION

Section (a):

1. You should make a clear distinction between statements and actions you engage in as a private individual and those you engage in as a representative of your profession, a professional social work organization, or your employing agency.

Section (b):

2. If you speak on behalf of a professional social work organization, you should accurately represent its official and authorized positions.

Section (c):

3. You should make sure that representations to clients, agencies, and the public of your professional qualifications, credentials, education, competence, affiliations, services provided, or results to be achieved are accurate.

4. You should claim only professional credentials you actually have.

5. You should take steps to correct any inaccuracies or misrepresentations of your credentials by others.

4.07 SOLICITATIONS

Section (a):

1. You should not engage in uninvited solicitation of potential clients who, due to their circumstances, are vulnerable to undue influence, manipulation, or coercion.

Section (b):

2. You should not engage in solicitation of testimonial endorsements from current clients or other individuals who, due to their particular circumstances, are vulnerable to undue influence. This standard also prohibits seeking consent from such a client or other individual to use his or her previous statements as testimonial endorsements.

4.08 ACKNOWLEDGING CREDIT

Section (a):

1. You should take credit and responsibility, including authorship credit, only for work you have actually performed and to which you have contributed.

2. You should honestly acknowledge the work of and contributions made by others.

5. ETHICAL RESPONSIBILITIES TO THE SOCIAL WORK PROFESSION

5.01 INTEGRITY OF THE PROFESSION

Section (a):

1. You should work toward the maintenance and promotion of high standards of social work practice.

Section (b):

2. You should uphold and promote the values, ethics, knowledge, and mission of your profession.

3. You should protect, enhance, and improve the integrity of your profession via appropriate study and research, active discussion, and responsible criticism.

Section (c):

4. You should contribute time and expertise to activities that foster respect for the value, integrity, and competence of the social work profession. For example, you might teach, do research, provide consultation, render services, provide legislative testimony, make presentations in the community, and participate in professional organizations.

Section (d):

5. You should contribute to the knowledge base of the social work profession.

6. You should share with colleagues your knowledge related to practice, research, and ethics.

7. You should strive to contribute to your profession's literature and to share your knowledge at professional meetings and conferences.

Section (e):

8. You should act to prevent the unauthorized and unqualified practice of social work.

5.02 EVALUATION AND RESEARCH

Section (a):

1. You should monitor and evaluate policies, the implementation of programs, and practice interventions.

Section (b):

2. You should promote and facilitate evaluation and research to contribute to the development of knowledge.

Section (c):

3. You should critically examine and keep current with new knowledge related to social work and fully use evaluation and research evidence in your professional practice.

Sections (d):

4. When in engaged in evaluation or research you should carefully consider possible consequences and should follow guidelines developed for the protection of evaluation and research participants. Appropriate institutional review boards should be consulted.

Section (e):

5. When engaged in evaluation or research you should obtain voluntary and written informed consent from participants, when appropriate, without any implied or actual deprivation or penalty for refusal to participate; without undue inducement to participate; and with due regard for participants' well-being, privacy, and dignity.

6. Informed consent should include information about the nature, extent, and duration of the participation requested and disclosure of the risks and benefits of participation in the research.

Section (f):

7. When using electronic technology to facilitate evaluation or research, you should ensure that participants provide informed consent for the use of such technology.

8. You should assess whether participants are able to use the technology and, when appropriate, offer reasonable alternatives to participate in the evaluation or research.

Section (g):

9. When evaluation or research participants are incapable of giving informed consent, you should provide an appropriate explanation to the participants, obtain the participants' assent to the extent they are able, and obtain written consent from an appropriate proxy.

Section (h):

10. You should never design or conduct evaluation or research that does not use consent procedures, such as certain forms of naturalistic observation and archival research, unless rigorous and responsible review of the research has found it to be justified because of its prospective scientific, educational, or applied value and unless equally effective alternative procedures that do not involve waiver of consent are not feasible.

Section (i):

11. You should inform participants of their right to withdraw from evaluation and research at any time without penalty.

Section (j):

12. You should take appropriate steps to ensure that participants in evaluation and research have access to appropriate supportive services.

Section (k):

13. When engaged in evaluation or research you should protect participants from unwarranted physical or mental distress, harm, danger, or deprivation.

Section (l):

14. When engaged in the evaluation of services you should discuss collected information only for professional purposes and only with people professionally concerned with this information.

Section (m):

15. When engaged in evaluation or research you should ensure the anonymity or confidentiality of participants and of the data obtained from them.

16. You should inform participants of any limits of confidentiality, the measures that will be taken to ensure confidentiality, and when any records containing research data will be destroyed.

Section (n):

17. When you report evaluation and research results you should protect participants' confidentiality by omitting identifying information unless proper consent has been obtained authorizing disclosure.

Section (o):

18. You should report evaluation and research findings accurately.

19. You should not fabricate or falsify results and should take steps to correct any errors later found in published data using standard publication methods.

Section (p):

20. When engaged in evaluation or research you should be alert to and avoid conflicts of interest and dual relationships with participants, you should inform participants when a real or potential conflict of interest arises, and should take steps to resolve the issue in a manner that makes participants' interests primary.

Section (q):

21. You should educate themselves, their students, and their colleagues about responsible research practices.

6. ETHICAL RESPONSIBILITIES TO THE BROADER SOCIETY

6.01 SOCIAL WELFARE

1. You should promote the general welfare of society, both locally and globally.

2. You should promote the development of people, their communities, and their environments.

3. You should advocate for living conditions that allow individuals to fulfill their basic human needs.

4. You should promote social, economic, political, and cultural values and institutions that facilitate the achievement of social justice.

6.02 PUBLIC PARTICIPATION

1. You should facilitate informed participation by the public in shaping social policies and institutions.

6.03 PUBLIC EMERGENCIES

1. You should provide appropriate professional services in public emergencies to the greatest degree possible.

6.04 SOCIAL AND POLITICAL ACTION

Section (a):

1. You should participate in social and political action that seeks to ensure all people have access to the resources, services, employment, and opportunities they need to meet their basic human needs and develop completely.

2. You should be aware of the effects of the political arena on your practice.

3. You should advocate for changes in policy and legislation that improve social conditions, so that social conditions will fulfill basic human needs and promote social justice.

Section (b):

4. You should act to increase choice and opportunity for all individuals, with special concern for vulnerable, disadvantaged, oppressed, and exploited persons and groups.

Section (c):

5. You should promote conditions that foster respect for cultural and social diversity within the U.S. and all over the world.

6. You should:

   a. promote policies and practices that demonstrate respect for differences;

   b. facilitate the expansion of cultural knowledge and resources;

   c. advocate for programs and institutions that exhibit cultural competence; and

   d. promote social policies that protect the rights of and affirm equity and social justice for all people.

Section (d):

7. You should act to prevent and end domination and exploitation of and discrimination against any individual, group, or class based on race, ethnicity, national origin, color, sex, sexual orientation, gender identity or expression, age, marital status, political belief, religion, immigration status, or mental or physical ability.

Appendix II: Professional Standards of the NASW

NASW has established numerous sets of professional standards which serve as important guidelines for professional social workers in a variety of practice settings. These standards include Standards for Continuing Professional Education; Standards for the Practice of Clinical Social Work; Standards for the Classification of Social Work Practice; Standards for the Practice of Social Work with Adolescents; Standards of Practice for Social Work Mediators; Standards for School Social Work Services; Standards for Social Work Case Management; Standards for Social Work in Health Care Settings; Standards for Social Work Personnel Practices; Standards for Social Work Practice in Child Protection; and Standards for Social Work Services in Long-Term Care Facilities. According to the NASW, you should interpret all of these standards within the ethical foundation and values expressed in the Code of Ethics.

In this Appendix, we excerpt and paraphrase many of the professional standards established by NASW. You should become familiar with the general requirements of these documents, but they are not as important for the exam as the NASW Code of Ethics.

NASW Standards for the Practice of Clinical Social Work

Standard 1: Clinical social workers function in accordance with the ethics and stated standards of the profession, including its accountability procedures.

1. NASW members are familiar with and follow the NASW Code of Ethics and professional standards for social work practice. They cooperate fully and in a timely manner with the adjudication processes of the Ethics Committee, peer review, and appropriate state boards.

2. Clinical social workers provide clients information about how to file a complaint charging unethical conduct when they request it.

Standard 2: Clinical social workers have and continue to develop specialized knowledge and understanding of individuals, families, and groups and of therapeutic and preventative interventions.

1. Clinical social workers have knowledge of the following areas:

    a. Social, psychological, and health factors and their interplay on psychosocial functioning.

    b. Social resources available in the community and their operation, how to use them on the client's behalf, and how to identify appropriate services and negotiate a referral.

    c. How to establish a relationship of mutual acceptance and trust, obtain, analyze, classify, and interpret social and personal information (including assessment and diagnosis), establish compatible goals of service with the client, and bring about changes in behavior or in the situation in accordance with the goals of service.

    d. Using research to evaluate the effectiveness of a service.

2. Clinical social workers know how to apply a variety of appropriate social work therapeutic intervention techniques and use them selectively depending on the client's needs and capacity for change.

3. When they acquire knowledge and skills, other than those specific to social work, clinical social workers obtain the appropriate training and certification.

4. Clinical social workers maintain and enhance their skills through appropriate forms of professional development and continuing education.

5. Clinical social workers are personally accountable for all aspects of their professional behavior and decisions.

Standard 3: Clinical social workers respond in a professional manner to all persons who seek their assistance.

1. Clinical social workers respond to each client regardless of the client's lifestyle, origin, race, sex, religion, or sexual orientation.

2. Clinical social workers limit their practice to those clients whom they have the skills and resources to serve. However, they are aware of and seek to improve any of their attitudes and practices that may interfere with their ability to offer competent and objective service.

3. Clinical social workers help a client establish contact with other appropriate resources when they cannot meet the needs of a particular client.

4. If clinical social workers are unable to schedule a timely appointment for an initial assessment, they may screen the client by telephone to determine the urgency of the client's situation. The well-being of the client is the key factor for all decisions.

5. For emergency situations in which clinical social workers cannot be available to a new client, they make every effort to find an appropriate source of immediate help for the client.

6. When a client insists on terminating treatment and the clinical social worker is certain that the termination is premature, the social worker refers the client to another appropriate treatment resource. Failing that, the social worker helps the client terminate treatment as constructively as possible, and leaves the door open for the client to reapply for service.

Standard 4: Clinical social workers are knowledgeable about the services available in the community and make appropriate referrals for their clients.

1. Clinical social workers are alert to a client's situation, especially when it affects the client's behavior and functioning.

2. Clinical social workers are able to modify their clients' environment when possible, by referrals to other community services. Advocacy on behalf of a client may be necessary to obtain needed services.

3. When a client is being served by other agencies, clinical social workers maintain collaborative contacts as necessary with the other providers to ensure the coordination of services and the clients' receipt of optimal benefits from the various services.

4. When a client is involved with more than one clinician, clinical social workers maintain collaborative consultation as necessary to ensure the delineation of the specific areas of responsibilities.

5. Clinical social workers do not share information about a client without the client's informed consent (See Standard 6).

Standard 5: Clinical social workers maintain their accessibility to clients.

1. Clinical social workers are able to respond to the unanticipated needs of a client; e.g., by having telephones answered, either by a person or machine, and the messages relayed promptly and accurately. These details are discussed with the client at the beginning of treatment.

2. When clinical social workers are unavailable because of vacation, illness, or any other reason, they make arrangements for coverage by competent peers. These details are discussed with the client at the beginning of treatment.

3. Because some clients have or develop physical handicaps, clinical social workers make every effort to ensure that their offices are free of obstacles to mobility and that helping devices are available for sensorially impaired clients.

4. When it is available, clinical social workers consider the office's accessibility by public transportation.

Standard 6: Clinical social workers safeguard the confidential nature of the treatment relationship and of the information obtained within that relationship.

1. A client is advised that there are circumstances in which confidentiality cannot be maintained. Along with others, these circumstances include the legally mandated requirement to report to appropriate authorities a suspicion of child abuse and to disclose information necessary to avert danger to the client or others, and the need to advise the parents when a minor client engages or is likely to engage in self-destructive behavior to ensure adequate protection for the child.

2. In all such circumstances, clinical social workers advise a client of the exceptions to confidentiality and privilege, are prepared to share with the client the information that is being reported, and handle the feelings evoked.

3. Except for explicit and overriding requirements, such as those listed above, clinical social workers share information only with the written and informed consent of the client.

Standard 7: Clinical social workers maintain access to professional case consultation.

1. In an agency setting, professional social work supervision or consultation is available to all social work staff, either in the agency or through a contractual arrangement. If clinical social workers are not available, case consultation may be obtained from qualified professionals from other disciplines.

2. For the first two years of professional experience, at least one hour of supervision is provided for every 15 hours of face-to-face contact with clients.

3. After the first two years, the ratio may be reduced to a minimum of one hour of case-consultation supervision for every 30 hours of face-to-face contact with clients.

Additional consultation may be sought by clinical social workers because of complex issues involving a client, or suggested by the consultant, because of difficulties the consultant perceives in a social worker's handling of the situation.

4. Clinical social workers with five years or more of experience utilize consultation on an as-needed, self determined basis.

5. Although clinical social workers who are in independent practice utilize more case consultation when they first begin practicing, they maintain consultative arrangements throughout the time they are in practice.

6. Clinical social workers are knowledgeable about how and when to use the expertise of other professional disciplines in the area of medical problems (including pharmacology) and are alert to the effects of prescription drugs so they can provide feedback to the client's physician.

Standard 8: Clinical social workers establish and maintain professional offices and procedures.

1. Clinical social workers keep records of clients that substantiate service in a secure place.

2. Clinical social workers maintain their records accurately and in a manner that is free from bias or prejudicial content.

3. Clinical social workers make these records available to clients at their request.

4. Clinical social workers ensure that appropriate insurance is maintained.

5. Clinical social workers establish a fee structure when in independent practice, or use the fee structure of the agency in which they are working.

6. All fees and payment procedures are discussed with the client at the beginning of treatment. (It is useful to present these policies in writing, as well.) The discussion includes the use of insurance reimbursement and how it will be handled, charges for missed or canceled appointments, vacations and collateral contacts, and any other financial issues.

7. Clinical social workers do not refuse service to a client just because the client is not covered by insurance.

8. Billing procedures are included in the original discussion, and client accounts are maintained in accordance to acceptable accounting methods, with all bills and receipts provided on a regular and timely schedule.

9. Clinical social workers discuss overdue accounts with clients and make every effort to avoid accumulation of debt.

10. When it is clear to a client and social worker that, for whatever reason, the client can no longer afford to pay for treatment, a mutually acceptable alternative plan for compensation or an orderly and appropriate termination or referral is instituted.

11. This standard is in no way intended to rule out the individual social worker's decision to provide services on a pro bono basis.

12. When all efforts to collect an overdue account from a client have failed, the client is informed that unpaid accounts may be turned over to a collection agency or small claims court or that other types of legal action will be taken.

13. If there is a dispute over charges, clinical social workers make every effort to resolve it without damaging the therapeutic relationship.

14. Waiting rooms and offices are kept clean, and the environment is properly maintained to ensure a reasonable degree of comfort.

15. Interviewing rooms ensure privacy and are free from distractions.

16. Steps are taken to assure the client's and social worker's personal security.

Standard 9: Clinical social workers represent themselves to the public with accuracy.

1. Because the public needs to know how to find help from qualified clinical social workers, agencies and independent private practitioners ensure that their therapeutic services are made known to the public.

2. Telephone listings are maintained in both the classified and alphabetical sections of the telephone directory, describing the clinical social work services available.

3. All advertisements are factual and avoid false promises of cures.

4. The content of the advertisement includes the private practitioner's or agency's name and professional credentials and the address and telephone number or other contact information. It might also include the type of services provided and the type or problems dealt with.

Standard 10: Clinical social workers engage in the independent private practice of clinical social work only when qualified to do so.

1. Many states have legal regulations for social workers at a clinical or independent-practice level. Practitioners who work in such a state are licensed or certified at this level to engage in independent private practice.

2. NASW standards for the independent practice of clinical social work are those required for inclusion in the NASW Register of Clinical Social Workers:

   a. a graduate degree from a social work program accredited by the Council on Social Work Education,

   b. two years of full-time (or equivalent part-time) clinical social work experience supervised by a clinical social worker, and

   c. current membership in the Academy of Certified Social Workers or a license or certification in a state at the appropriate level.

Standard 11: Clinical social workers have the right to establish an independent private practice.

1. Clinical social workers have the right to establish a separate independent practice as a form of secondary employment or after leaving a place of employment.

2. When clinical social workers establish such a practice, either alone or as part of a group, they assure that the diagnostic and treatment services meet professional standards.

3. If clinicians who establish such a practice hire clinical social workers or other employees, they, as employers, are responsible for the services provided, for maintaining all these standards, and for upholding all applicable local, state, or federal regulations.

4. Clinical social workers who are employed by agencies and have an independent practice do not refer agency clients to themselves unless they have made a specific agreement with the agency and offered alternative options to the clients.

5. Agencies have the responsibility to establish written, reasonable guidelines or policies about secondary employment. When an agency does not have clear written policies, clinical social workers may cite the relevant NASW standards.

6. When clinical social workers leave an agency to establish an independent private practice, they take great care to explain fully the options available to clients. Clients in treatment may be offered various options after consultation with the agency, including transferring to another staff member in the agency; continuing with the same clinician in an independent setting; transferring to another agency or different private practitioner; or terminating treatment. The overriding principle is the client's right to self-determination and freedom of choice. That is, the client's best interests are always paramount in these decisions.

NASW Standards for Continuing Professional Education

Continuing education is training taken by social workers and other professionals who have already completed the formal education required to begin working in their field. Most professions require their members to keep up with the current knowledge base by participating in specified additional trainings within certain time limits. The goal of continuing education is to develop one's professional skills and improve one's professional competence.

The Code of Ethics includes a specific standard related to competence and continued enhancement of your social work skills. NASW's Task Force on Standards for Continuing Professional Education is responsible for reviewing the current state of continuing education as provided by schools, professional organizations, and agencies. In addition, NASW provides funding grants to encourage the development of continuing education programs, and often schools and agencies in the community collaborate to develop these programs.

The NASW Standards for Continuing Professional Education include the following provisions:

Standards for Social Workers: As a social worker you shall:

1. Assume personal responsibility for your continuing professional education;

2. complete forty-eight hours of continuing professional education every two years; and

3. contribute to the development and improvement of continuing professional education.

Standards for Assessing Providers of Continuing Professional Education: Providers of continuing professional education shall:

1. Have a written statement of mission and philosophy which reflects the values and ethics of the social work profession;

2. plan an organized educational experience;

3. conform to responsible administrative practices; and

4. collaborate with NASW chapters and local accredited programs of social work education in developing their offerings.

Standards for Administrators: Administrators shall:

1. Implement agency policies in support of continuing professional education; and

2. provide leadership for continuing professional education.

NASW Standards for the Practice of Social Work With Adolescents

The professional social worker who works with adolescents:

1. Shall demonstrate knowledge and understanding of adolescent development (Standard 1).

2. Shall demonstrate an understanding of and ability to: assess the needs of adolescents; assess social institutions, organizations, and resources for adolescents and their families; and advocate for the development of needed resources (Standard 2).

3. Shall demonstrate knowledge and understanding of family dynamics (Standard 3).

4. Shall demonstrate acceptance of and contribute to the development of and maintenance of culturally competent service delivery (Standard 4).

5. Shall have or have access to specialized knowledge of the legal, regulatory, and administrative requirements and resources for youths and their families (Standard 5).

6. Shall strive to empower adolescents (Standard 6).

7. Shall advocate for an understanding of the needs of adolescents and for resources and cooperation among professionals and agencies to meet those needs (Standard 7).

8. Shall participate in multidisciplinary case consultation across agencies that provide services to adolescents and their families (Standard 8).

9. Shall maintain confidentiality in their relationship with youths and of the information obtained within that relationship (Standard 9).

10. Shall assume an active role in contributing to the improvement and quality of the work, environment, agency policies and practices with clients, and their own professional development (Standard 10).

NASW Standards of Practice for Social Work Mediators

In "mediation," a form of conflict resolution, a neutral third person helps two parties in opposition come to a mutually acceptable and informed resolution. The mediator is someone who has been accepted by both sides. His or her job is to improve communication between the parties, help them explore their options as fully as possible, and address the needs of the parties and others who may be affected by the issues at hand. Ultimately, the mediator seeks to empower the parties by providing them structure and the tools they need to reach an agreement. The goal is to enable the parties to come to a resolution on their own. In this way, they can avoid having to go to court or arbitration to make their decision.

NASW's Standards of Practice for Social Work Mediators include the following standards:

The professional social work mediator:

1. Shall function within the ethics and stated standards and accountability procedures of the social work profession (Standard 1).

2. Shall remain impartial and neutral toward all parties and issues in a dispute (Standard 2).

3. Must not reveal to outside parties any information revealed in the mediation process (Standard 3).

4. Must assess each conflict and shall proceed only in those circumstances in which mediation is an appropriate procedure (Standard 4).

5. Shall seek at all times to promote cooperation, to prevent the use of coercive tactics, to foster good-faith bargaining efforts, and to ensure that all agreements are arrived at on a voluntary and informed basis (Standard 5).

6. Shall recommend termination of the process when it appears that it is no longer in the interest of the parties to continue it (Standard 6).

7. Is responsible for helping the parties arrive at a clearly stated, mutually understood, and mutually acceptable agreement (Standard 7).

8. Shall develop an unbiased written agreement that specifies the issues resolved during the course of the mediation (Standard 8).

9. Must have training in both the procedural and substantive aspects of mediation (Standard 9).

10. Shall have a fair and clearly defined fee structure (Standard 10).

11. Shall not use any information obtained during the mediation process for personal benefit or for the benefit of any group or organization with which the mediator is associated (Standard 11).

12. Must be prepared to work collaboratively as appropriate with other professionals and in conformance to the philosophy of social work and mediation (Standard 12).

NASW Standards for School Social Work Services

Standards of Competence and Professional Practice: A school social worker:

1. Shall demonstrate commitment to the values and ethics of the social work profession and shall use NASW's professional standards and Code of Ethics as a guide to ethical decision-making (Standard 1).

2. As a leader or member of an interdisciplinary team, shall work collaboratively to mobilize the resources of the local education agencies and the community to meet the needs of children and families (Standard 2).

3. Shall develop and provide training and educational programs that address the goals and mission of the educational institution (Standard 3).

4. Must organize his or her time, energies, and work loads to fulfill his or her responsibilities and complete assignments with due consideration of the priorities among his or her various responsibilities (Standard 4).

5. Shall maintain accurate data that are relevant to the planning, management, and evaluation of the school social work program (Standard 5).

6. Is responsible for identifying individual children and target populations in need of services; he or she does so through a process of needs assessment that includes planned consultation with personnel of the local education agency, community representatives, and children and their families (Standard 6).

7. Shall know how to use objective measures and shall integrate them into his or her evaluation and subsequent development of reports, when appropriate (Standard 7).

8. Following an assessment, shall develop and implement a plan of intervention, or when the most suitable intervention is not available, shall develop an alternative plan that will enhance the child's ability to benefit from his or her educational experience (Standard 8).

9. As systems change agents, shall identify areas of need that are not being addressed by the local education agency and community and shall work to create those services (Standard 9).

10. Must provide consultation to personnel of the local education agency, members of school boards, and representatives of the community to promote understanding and the effective use of school social work services (Standard 10).

11. Shall ensure that children and their families are provided services within the context of multicultural understanding and sensitivities that enhance the families' support of the children's learning experiences (Standard 11).

12. Shall extend their services to children in ways that build on the children's individual strengths and that offer them maximum opportunity to participate in the planning and direction of their own learning experiences (Standard 12).

13. Shall empower children and their families to gain access to and effectively use formal and informal community resources (Standard 13).

14. Must maintain adequate safeguards for the privacy and confidentiality of information (Standard 14).

15. Shall be trained in and use mediation and conflict-resolution strategies to resolve children's educational problems (Standard 15).

16. Shall advocate for children and their families in a variety of situations (Standard 16).

Standards of Professional Preparation and Development: A school social worker:

1. Shall have knowledge and understanding that are basic to the social work profession and specialized knowledge and understanding of the local education agency, of the process of education, and of relevant legislation and due process (Standard 17).

NASW Standards for Social Work Case Management

Significant provisions of NASW's Standards for Social Work Case Management include the following:

The social work case manager:

1. Shall use his or her professional skills and competence to serve the client whose interests are of primary concern (Standard 2).

2. Shall ensure that clients are involved in all phases of case management practice to the greatest extent possible (Standard 3).

3. Shall ensure the client's right to privacy and ensure appropriate confidentiality when information about the client is released to others (Standard 4).

4. Shall intervene at the client level to provide and/or coordinate the delivery of direct services to the client and his or her family (Standard 5).

5. Shall intervene at the service systems level to support existing case management services and to expand the supply of and improve access to needed services (Standard 6).

6. Shall be knowledgeable about resource availability, service costs, and budgetary parameters and be fiscally responsible in carrying out all case management functions and activities (Standard 7).

7. Shall participate in evaluative and quality assurance activities designed to monitor the appropriateness and effectiveness of both the service delivery system in which case management operates as well as the case manager's own case management services, and to otherwise ensure full professional accountability (Standard 8).

8. Shall carry a reasonable caseload that allows him or her to effectively plan, provide, and evaluate case management tasks related to client and system interventions (Standard 9).

9. Shall ... strive to enhance interprofessional, intraprofessional, and interagency cooperation on behalf of the client (Standard 10).

NASW Standards for Social Work in Health-Care Settings

According to this document, "Social work services shall be an integral part of every health-care organization. The services shall be provided to individuals, their families, and significant others; to special populations groups; to communities; and to special health-related programs and educational systems.

To provide comprehensiveness and continuity of care, social work services [in health-care settings] shall encompass the following:

1. The promotion and maintenance of physical and psychosocial well-being.

2. The promotion of conditions essential to assure maximum benefits from short-and long-term care services.

3. The prevention of physical or mental illness.

4. The promotion and enhancement of physical and psychosocial functioning, with attention to the social and emotional impact of illness or disability.

5. The promotion of ethical responses to address the often conflicting value positions held by various parties involved in health-care settings."

NASW Standards for Social Work Practice in Child Protection

Among others, this document contains the following statement: "The Standards presented in this section [VI, Standards for workers of agencies providing child protective services] document the practice expectations of social workers throughout the various phases of direct intervention. These expectations, when actively supported by administrators and supervisors, enable social workers to carry out their responsibilities to: families and parents, children, the agency, and the community. Written documentation of all intervention activities is implicit in meeting the requirements of these Standards."

Important standards included in this document include the following:

The Social Worker's Responsibility to Families and Children: The social worker providing child protective services:

    1. Shall be responsive to reports of suspected child abuse and neglect (Standard 17).

    2. Shall competently assess the parent's ability and willingness to protect the child (Standard 18).

    3. Shall engage the family in using its own strengths and resources throughout the service planning process (Standard 19).

    4. Shall provide direct and intensive services to parents to strengthen their capacity to care for their children (Standard 20).

    5. Shall be prepared to initiate and follow through on court action on the child's behalf (Standard 21).

    6. Shall use social work processes in the termination of services to a family (Standard 22).

    7. Shall manage the personal feelings associated with providing child protective services (Standard 23).

The Social Worker's Responsibility to Endangered Children: The social worker providing child protective services:

    1. Shall continuously assess the presence and level of risk to all children in the family (Standard 24).

    2. Shall engage in ongoing service planning to maintain or to reunite children with their own families (Standard 25).

    3. Shall ensure that endangered children participate in the planning and direction of their lives (Standard 26).

    4. Shall pursue permanency planning for children and shall initiate action to terminate parental rights, as necessary (Standard 27).

    5. Shall consistently work toward the enhancement of resources for children within the agency and community (Standard 28).

The Social Worker's Responsibility to the Community: The social worker providing child protective services:

1. Shall promote collaborative working relationships among community agencies and the court toward establishment of a comprehensive child protective system (Standard 35).

2. Shall strive to prevent child abuse and neglect by promoting resources in the community to support and strengthen the family unit (Standard 36).

Standards for the Social Worker Employed in a Setting Other Than Child Protective Services: "All social workers have professional responsibility for supplementing the efforts of agencies providing child protective services in the identification, assessment, treatment, and prevention of child abuse and neglect." The social worker:

1. Shall acquire knowledge about child abuse and neglect, the agencies and local process, and child welfare services (Standard 37).

2. Shall comply with child abuse and neglect reporting laws and procedures (Standard 38).

3. Shall share responsibility with other workers providing services to endangered children and their families (e.g., joint case planning and service delivery, provision of consultation services) (Standard 39).

4. Shall advocate for community services to protect children, strengthen families, and prevent child abuse and neglect (Standard 40).

NASW Standards for Social Work in Long-Term Care Facilities

In this context, "long-term care facilities" include skilled nursing facilities, intermediate or health-related care facilities, and residential care facilities. According to these standards, "Social work services in long-term care settings focus on the social and emotional impact of physical or mental illness or disability, the preservation and enhancement of physical and social functioning, the promotion of those conditions essential to assure maximum benefits from long-term health-care services, the prevention of physical and mental illness and increased disability or dysfunction, and the promotion and maintenance of physical and mental health and an optimal quality of life."

Social work objectives include the following:

1. Providing direct social services to residents, their families, and significant others.

2. Assisting residents, families, and significant others to utilize appropriately and receive maximum benefit from the facility and community-based social and health resources on a continuum throughout the stay of each individual from preadmission to discharge or death.

3. Strengthening communications between residents, their families, and significant others, and the program or facility staff.

4. Assisting the facility to achieve and maintain a therapeutic environment essential to the optimal quality of life and independent functioning of each resident and to provide for maximum participation of residents in planning activities and policies.

5. Promoting facility-community interaction through encouraging community involvement in the facility and resident and staff involvement in the community, developing linkages with a wide range of community resources, and participating in the assessment of the need for and planning of other long-term social and health-care resources.